# WITNESSES WANTED

# WITNESSES WANTED

## Living an UNEXPECTED Adventurous Life

### JOHAN GOUS

NASHVILLE

NEW YORK • LONDON • MELBOURNE • VANCOUVER

# WITNESSES **WANTED**
## Living an UNEXPECTED Adventurous Life

Published in New York, New York, by Morgan James Publishing. Morgan James is a trademark of Morgan James, LLC. www.MorganJamesPublishing.com

ISBN 978-1-64279-256-0 paperback
ISBN 978-1-64279-257-7 eBook
Library of Congress Control Number: 2018910584

**Cover Design by:**
Rachel Lopez
www.r2cdesign.com

**Interior Design by:**
Bonnie Bushman
The Whole Caboodle Graphic Design

**Edited by:**
John Lindner

In an effort to support local communities, raise awareness and funds, Morgan James Publishing donates a percentage of all book sales for the life of each book to Habitat for Humanity Peninsula and Greater Williamsburg.

Get involved today! Visit
www.MorganJamesBuilds.com

# CONTENTS

# FOREWORD

**Who is this man?**
This question is not about the author. It was first asked more than 2000 years ago by Mary and Joseph, the parents of Jesus: Who is this child? And when Jesus visited the temple at 12 years of age, the scribes in the temple similarly wondered (Luke 2).

**Who is this Jesus?**
John the Baptist also asked, "Are you the one?" (Matthew 11:3, NIV). When Jesus' feet were anointed, the Pharisees asked, "Who is this who even forgives sins?" (Luke.7:49, NIV). The religious leaders of his day were offended when He said to the paralyzed man, "My child, your sin is forgiven" (Mark 2:5, NLT). When Jesus rode into Jerusalem on a donkey, the populace also asked, "Who is this?" (Matthew 21:10). Jesus Himself asked the disciples, "Who do you say that I am?" and Peter gave

the testimony of all ages when he confessed, "You are the Christ, the Son of the living God!" (Matthew 16:16, ESV). After Jesus rose from the dead, Thomas affirmed the confession when he cried out, "My Lord and my God" (John 20:28, NIV).

That confession turned into a movement. Witnesses told how God reconciled the world to Himself through Jesus, and that they could have their sins forgiven through Him. The evidence was so compelling that the same question was asked about those who testified, "Who are these people?"

At the outpouring of the Holy Spirit, people from 14 language groups wondered, Who are these people? Gamaliel warned the Jewish council about acting against them, lest they be found working against God (Acts. 5.37ff). Pursuing Christians to persecute them, Saul was stopped by Jesus Himself on the road to Damascus. Stricken blind, he asks, "Who are You, Lord?" (Acts. 9:5, NIV).

Thus, "this Man" raised questions from the very beginning. This Jesus left just 12 disciples behind as His last will and testament, and they began making disciples so aggressively that the world again asked, "Who are these people?" He used them ultimately to change millions of lives.

These people did not consider their lives too important to carry the message to all people. They were prepared to proclaim His story until death—even martyrdom. They took the word to all who were near and to all who were far away (Eph. 2:17, NIV)—people who became disciples and followers of Jesus Christ and each other, and who kept making disciples despite opposition, suffering, distress, hunger, persecution, danger and death. They made disciples because this command was not only a command and a calling (Matthew 28:19) but also a work that became a natural outcropping of their changed nature (1Cor. 9:16-18, NIV).

This autobiography deals with one of "these people"—a disciple who simply heard the call and asked very few questions, who started going out of obedience and shared the good news, a disciple whose actions empowered many others. He started helping indigenous missionaries and teachers, and that led to empowering disciples to be disciples-who-make-disciples. This book tells of human suffering, but with divine perseverance, a person who ran the race to get the prize of glory on that day when we will see the King in glory (1Cor.9:26, NIV).

Who is this author? Just another disciple. A disciple known to many in Africa as "Papa Johan." He is neither a high-ranking person nor a beggar, but simply a commoner who became a disciple of Jesus. Perhaps "spiritual grandfather" would be an appropriate designation—the greatest recognition that a disciple can receive in Africa (or on this earth).

Read through this story, ponder every hardship and hurt. Wonder at the outcome and why it happened. Pause at every victory as well as each suffering and hurt, and worship the God who remains faithful to His called people. There was (and always is) power to endure, and Light drives out the darkness every time.

This is not just a story or the history of a human being. That's merely the shell! This book will help you evaluate your own stance before God. Are you a disciple? Are you part of "these people" who follow "this Man," Jesus, and cannot stop talking about Him?

If you are, sharing the hurt and hardships, rejoicing together in Christ's victory in Africa and other continents will become natural. Then, and maybe only then, if this honor is bestowed on you, "this Man" will compel you to leave everything behind, to make a difference in the lives of people in Jerusalem, Judea, Samaria and the uttermost parts of the earth.

If you are waiting for a specific call or sign to get involved somewhere, you have missed the point. The specific call is the willingness to commit. Above all, this testimony is a call to "engage" for anyone who believes that "this Man" is the Christ.

Read the book. Study the source—the Bible—and be energized to live a life not only of a disciple, but of a disciple-maker.

Rev. David Fourie
Friend and colleague

# PREFACE

Looking back over a life changed dramatically by the call of God leaves me no alternative but to write this account in the first person. My goal is two-fold: First, to be a witness of God's grace and mercy to ordinary people who choose to be His followers and second, to encourage people like you to step out obediently and experience for yourself that God's promise in Matthew 6:33 is true: "Seek first the kingdom of God and his righteousness, and all these things will be added unto you" (ESV).

In our walk with Christ as Savior and Lord as a family and ministry, we consistently apply two basic principles: P.U.S.H. (Pray Until Something Happens) and, equip, empower and encourage people as God, through His Spirit, directs us.

The road was not always smooth or easy, but through it all we can testify (sometimes only in retrospect) that God never forsook or abandoned us. It is my prayer that your life experience will be similarly impacted as you dedicate yourself to serve Him who rescues everyone who believes and provides Living Water flowing from you to a hungry and thirsty world (John 7:38).

It is also necessary to note that missionary families come under scrutiny from all sides as they endeavor to represent Christ in what they do. This brings pressure to bear on their children, and consequently, parents are held to a higher standard by the community for their children's behavior. "After all, they are the pastor's kids." Yet I trust you know why they are naughty sometimes: They play with the kids of church members.

God instituted the family as the basic building block of society through whom He wants to display Himself to the world. A Christian family living out the values of Christ as revealed in Scripture can prevail in the spiritual battle called life. Without my wife Lida's faith, unwavering support, and encouragement, none of the adventures you will read about would have been possible. Seriously, the battle in the heavenly realm is real, and only if and when our armor is worn and fits well are we able to withstand the temptations, frustrations, and heartaches that we will meet on our journey through this life and remain standing in victory, to His glory. His promise is true: "For God has said, 'I will never fail you. I will never abandon you'" (Hebrews 13:5 NLT).

In this adventure, our family has remained unified, all glory to God. We have three daughters and three sons-in-law, and all six are immersed in ministry. We also intensely intercede, for God's grace, mercy and favor, on behalf of our 11 grandkids. Although they are growing up in different environments, they all face the challenges influencing their life choices.

Well down the road in the second half of my life, I like to share three truths with people God brings me:

The first is that only "in Christ" do we inherit true life and all the associated promises of God.

Second, it is a relationship of *trust* (not just *understanding*) and a *walk in obedience to the guidance of the Holy Spirit* that allows us to become representatives (disciple-makers) of Christ in this world.

And third, *life choices based on godly values really matter.*

# ^^^1 WHERE IT ALL BEGAN

I was born on a farm in the arid Highveld of South Africa not far from the edge of the Kalahari (semi-desert). Chores included collecting the eggs from chicken coops and washing them, tending to cattle and sheep as they grazed, and driving tractors during the planting seasons. All of this taught my older brother and me early on the lessons about what real life was all about—hard work, responsibility, vigilance, love for the land, and discipline. Our education started in a two-room farm school for grades 1 through 7. The next step was to go in town to high school (grades 8 to 12). Fortunately, Mom worked in town, so we did not need to go to boarding school, but we could commute to town daily and still live at home.

By the time I had finished grade 7, Father's health had deteriorated. He suffered from calcification of the tubes in his lungs caused by the fine airborne dust particles brought on by dynamite blasting in the gold mines. Doctors advised him to move to a more humid climate.

Port Shepstone on the east coast became our new home—right on the Indian Ocean.

The problem for us boys was that there was no Afrikaans medium (mother language tuition) school in Port Shepstone. We could go to a boarding school in a city some two hours away and be taught in our mother tongue, or go to one of the two high schools in town where all instruction was in English. We chose the latter. It was a delightful choice, enabling us to enjoy the beaches, the bodyboarding, and fishing—not to mention meeting the young ladies who vacationed there.

Graduating from high school in 1968 brought another challenge. A couple of my friends and I had decided to study law. Lawyers make money, right? And we had already been accepted at the university. But after some soul-searching, I concluded that I was not ready to follow a life of constantly dealing with the dark side of humanity. This realization came after I spent some time at the home of one of my friends whose father was a trial attorney.

My parents were diligently making all the arrangements for me to go to the university 500 miles inland. I had to decide quickly, and I decided to consider another line of work for a career. (The thought of staying near the ocean with its fun and frolic might have played a role.)

An opening in the electrical division of the local sugar mill looked like an opportunity. The mill offered to send me to college for six months of every year of my apprenticeship, after which I would do my practical training under a mentor in the electrical shop. I could stay at my parents' home and enjoy good food, laundry facilities and, of course, the ocean. The Technical Institute in our small town had an agreement with the sugar mill; within a few days arrangements were flipped, and I was happy with the results.

I was assigned to a qualified electrician as an apprentice. He was an accomplished mentor, which yielded a strong relationship. His way of doing things was the way I did them, also. The strength of this method of teaching impressed me deeply. These principles, theoretical training followed by practically implementing what I had learned, would serve me well in later years in ministry. I later thought along these lines while grappling with serious obstacles in the most remote places in Africa where God would call us to serve. Challenges such as low literacy, untrained leaders and poor infrastructure would call for innovative solutions. God used this apprenticeship model to overcome many obstacles.

I spent quite a bit of time praying about both the pulling out of the law career and going into engineering. My parents had a policy that continued to shape my life and that of my children: "We will support you in your decisions, but when you start something, you finish it." So, I had to make sure that engineering was where I wanted to be for the rest of my life. Now, many years later, I see how God directed my steps for what He knew lay ahead of me should I follow His guidance. Of course, I was oblivious to the bigger picture that was taking shape—preparation for a call to ministry.

Another huge shift in my worldview came at that time. Together with my family, I had grown up attending church. I knew answers to faith questions, but an emptiness persisted in my heart. Our local pastor had an interview with each of the young men and women in 11th grade to talk to us about our faith. His question, "How certain are you that your relationship with Christ will stand the assault by the worldly temptations? Can you clearly say that you love Jesus so much that what you have learned about Him will keep you from participating in worldly activities?"

That drove my struggle with vacillating between "good and evil" to the forefront. I could not responsibly answer in the affirmative. He took a small vase with a lip curled inward, put a marble in and swirled it around. The marble did not fly out because that lip stopped it from doing so. This, he explained is what happens to us if we become children of God—our lives in Christ are shielded from evil and sin as long as we follow the guidance of the Holy Spirit. I got it. Understanding that I could not trade on the faith of my parents became clear; my relationship had to be personal—we serve a personal God.

Later I would find out that my wife Lida had gone through the same struggle. She also learned that growing up in church did not allow her to skate past judgment on the faith of her parents; she had to surrender personally to a life in relationship with Christ.

But siding with God does not necessarily enable us to avoid difficulties—or even tragedies.

Only a short while after really starting to intentionally follow Christ, the question, "Where was God?" confronted me. A new pastor accepted the call to our local congregation and, being a deacon, I went to pick up some of the cakes and snacks for the reception from members of my ward. On the way, I was involved in a severe head-on collision. My little Mini had an argument with a Chrysler Valiant—from a pure size and momentum point of view, we lost the encounter. The engine of my Mini was pushed back close to the passenger seat. With the abrupt stop, the car behind me demolished the rear-end of my car, sandwiching me between the two bigger cars. My car's steering wheel was bent up towards the broken windshield, and the doors would not open. The space around the driver's seat, however, was about the only area that was still semi in-tact! Although three cars were total losses, nobody was seriously injured. I managed to climb out and sat on the curb, waiting for the police to arrive.

I finally realized that following Christ costs a price. Satan, the enemy of our souls, does not easily give up territory he once claimed. It became clear that the question was not "Where was God?" That was the wrong question; it was He who had protected me. The question I had to come to grips with was, "Where was I in my walk with Christ?" Although I prayed for God's protection, it did not "guarantee" immunity from adversity.

I had some irritation stemming from the intrusion of the church activity into my Saturday, and it had caused me to have a less than good attitude. I do not believe that there is a direct cause and effect link between the two situations but reflecting on the overall circumstances taught me how important a "clean heart" before God was. Prompted by the Holy Spirit, the dilemma helped me confess, repent, and ask for forgiveness and restoration of an open relationship with Christ. This has remained an ongoing principle in my life.

After three years as an apprentice, I graduated with honors as well as with hands-on, practical experience as a Junior Electrical Engineer. With my time at the sugar mill done, I was ready to spread my wings to explore the world and start the career that was out there for me. It began three days later when I called the number of a very large international company in response to an advertisement in a national newspaper for an "electrical motor specialist." When I mentioned that I had physically worked in all divisions of a sugar mill, the voice of the lady taking notes from respondents to the advertisement changed markedly. She transferred me immediately to a Mr. Schultz, the General Manager. He asked, "How quickly can you be in my office for an interview?" "Two hours," I blurted out. It would take me that long to drive, and I still had to dress to meet a possible employer.

I was on time, the short interview went well, and I was hired— but not as an electric motor specialist. They hired me to assist Project Engineers working in the sugar industry. However, when I started, I was put into another division. I never got to work on sugar projects but was deployed in the most exciting discipline in engineering—Ship Building. This included systems design, construction and commissioning. In ten years in that capacity, I learned more about life than at any time before. I worked with sailors (often from different countries) and engineers from all different trades, crammed into the compressed spaces of a ship, working against deadlines. This all made life a constant battle to remain ahead of the pack, get your work done as fast as possible and stay out of the way of others (unless you wanted to get into confrontations that could get more than just nasty).

Having workers in multiple spaces in the ship required me to supervise many projects concurrently. I needed to know what each area needed and what vendors could meet those needs. I developed multitasking skills that were valuable going forward. The cross-cultural relationships I had embraced, having workers from all over the world on the contract, was another building block in preparation for what lay ahead, as was the capacity of accommodating vendors in tight spaces and working under stressful conditions.

In 1975, I was introduced to Lida. She was a Sunday School teacher at the church my parents attended. I was on the relief staff and substituted in classes when needed. After Sunday school I looked for her, but she did not stay for the service. Later I learned that she had gone to visit her great aunt—an effective intercessor, who had prayed with her and comforted her when she learned that her father had been diagnosed with cancer. Knowing only her name, I had to figure out how to contact her. I called a teacher friend who also taught at the local high school, and he connected us. I asked Lida whether she would be open for a coffee and waffle. She agreed, and we enjoyed the afternoon together.

On our way back from the beach I stopped in at my parents' home to gather my stuff to go back to my residence in the city—so she was introduced to my parents. After dropping her off at her apartment, I drove straight over to the house of my best friend who had connected us to tell him that he needed to get his best suit ready because I had just met my wife. At our wedding three months later, I found out that Lida had written to her best friend, Rosie, that same evening telling her that she was sure "this was the one" and asked to be her attendant at the wedding.

Fully immersed in my work as a Project Engineer on several ships in various stages of completion, I was more than happy with the development of my career and family life. Lida was teaching at a school near our first, very modest home. With both of us working we established our lives so that when our first child came along, Lida could be a stay-at-home mom. Our firm desire was to build and maintain strong, familial bonds. We both had actively participated in our churches from a young age and continued to do so in our married life.

Brother Andrew (also known as God's Smuggler) came to our city later in 1976. He took Bibles and needed encouragement into places where Christians were being persecuted and martyred for their faith. Our hearts responded to his message. The stories he told of the experiences he had in obeying the guidance of the Holy Spirit awakened in me a desire to have that same faith. We joined a local Open Doors prayer group to intercede for those brothers and sisters who faithfully proclaimed the gospel of Jesus Christ in their restrictive communities, despite the dangers to their lives. By mid-1977 I was asked to substitute (when needed) on a team that visited ships in the Durban harbor going to countries "closed to the gospel." Not long after this, I became a regular member of that outreach team.

The prayer group grew into a discipleship group which was of great importance to our spiritual growth. It became a renewal movement— Christians believing that it took more than religion to be genuine followers of Christ. It required more than a one-hour Sunday morning service, more than reading a piece in the Bible, more than a short prayer before bedtime. Walking in faith with Jesus meant discerning and obeying God's will in daily life to become mature followers and witnesses of Christ. Only then could we see our prayers answered, and teach with authority (like Jesus, not like the Pharisees). We had to walk the walk as well as talk the talk. As Lida and I grew in our faith, we were reminded of how God led us individually to understand that God has no grandchildren. There is no substitute for a personal relationship with Jesus.

*Lida's perspective:* *This growth to maturity was very new and, in a way, scary to me. We were so set in our ways and the formal and non-demonstrative way of worship practices in our denomination that it took a while before I was free to act and enjoy worship with no regard for what others thought of me. We had grown into a freedom to become our unique selves and act as the Holy Spirit led us, being aware only of His Presence.*

∨ ∨ ∨

# 2 TAKING THE FIRST STEP — VOLUNTEERING IN THE HARBOR MINISTRY

A s the junior member of the Harbor Ministry Team, my role was to help carry Bibles and other materials we used when we talked with crew members who were off duty on Sunday mornings. When we identified ships on routes to or from countries where the Bible was considered contraband, we would find out whether there were Christians on board. If not, we would seek to do evangelism by asking if the sailors would be interested in hearing about Jesus. The conversations took place in the mess (dining room) where the off-duty sailors relaxed. Many times, "interested men" would exit the mess as we were ready to leave. We soon found out why. As we walked down the hallways, cabin doors would open, and a hand would grab a Bible. Crew members from "closed countries" feared being targeted by on-board commissars who would report them to authorities at home. In this way, many Bibles got into the hands of men whom we never saw or spoke to again.

Team members Willie and Elsa led the evangelism discussions quietly to protect the men showing an interest. This allowed me to learn how to sensitively recruit Christians to take Bibles into countries where they were not available to believers. Pointing out that we as Christians all have the call to be witnesses of Christ and that believers in many countries could not get a Bible usually was enough to motivate them to answer our plea for help. Thousands of Bibles were sent into "closed countries" through these couriers. They did not need to go through Customs when they left their ships and interacted with people wherever they went.

Three significant encounters remain fresh in my mind:

On a ship with an Iranian crew, we met and spoke to a young man, Baktiar. He knew the name of Jesus but was very interested in learning about the "how" of Jesus being the Son of God and therefore Himself God. He listened and read the passages Willie shared. When we left, he promised to read the Bible we left with him. His ship had to off-load cargo in a port some two days away and then return to Durban to take on new cargo. We knew the lady in Port Elizabeth who did similar outreach work there, so we alerted her of his coming. She undertook to visit him when he was available. She reported back that her time with him had been very fruitful. She also informed him that we would call on him upon his return to Durban.

Our prayers were answered out on the high seas between Port Elizabeth and Durban. He shared with great enthusiasm, "I fell into deep desperation earlier in my life; I had many problems at home. That led me to apply for a job that would take me away from there for long periods of time. I followed the instructions for prayer given by our Imam, but I still felt empty with no change in my situation. I was desperate. With what you had taught me about the promises of God in Jesus as Savior, I went out on the back deck ready to commit suicide if God could not free me from this feeling of desperation and guilt.

I prayed, 'God, Jesus, if you are real, please reveal yourself to me and answer my prayer for forgiveness.' Instantly I was aware of the presence of a 'warm, great peace all around.' I knew Jesus answered my prayer.'"

We saw him twice more, encouraging him to stand firm in light of the possible negative reaction of family and friends when he declared his faith back home. As his ship sailed out into the night, he sang the song we had taught him: "I have decided to follow Jesus, no turning back, no turning back." That was the last we ever heard from Baktiar. We did, however, continue praying for him for a very long time.

I met Pakr, a Korean on the *Princess Esmeralda*. In reply to my inquiry about Christians on the vessel, a deckhand said that there was one Christian on board, the boatswain Pakr. His understanding of English and mine of Korean were about at the same level. We exchanged greetings by pointing out verses we could read in our own Bibles. After a while, he called an officer who did speak English but was not a believer to help us communicate with understanding. As a brother, I invited them to come to our Wednesday evening service.

Pakr accepted if he could bring three officers with him—men he was witnessing to. Before the service, Pakr asked to see the inside of our church. Great was Pakr's enthusiasm when he saw the big pipe organ— he had not seen one like ours before. Lida sat down and started playing "Silent Night," and when he recognized the music, he started singing at full volume. Both Lida and I joined him singing in our native language. The impact of this display of "family" (as the other officers termed it) made such an impact on them that when we took them back to their ship that night, we had three more brothers in Christ.

Pakr and I exchanged birthday cards for several years. I must admit I never learned enough Korean to understand the messages in those cards, but I knew they came from his heart to mine, and that was sufficient.

A professor at the naval academy in Vladivostok, Russia undertook one voyage every year to keep his Commander's license updated.

On a voyage past the east coast of South Africa, he developed severe appendicitis. As the medical officer on the vessel, he knew how serious his condition was. The Captain refused to contact South African authorities for help; he did not want an officer unaccompanied in an "anti-Communist" country. As the situation became critical, his only option was to operate on himself with the aid of mirrors. At that point, the Captain relented, and the Professor was airlifted to a hospital (which we regularly monitored for foreign sailors).

We met him days after his surgery, and for a week we had a lot of time to spend with him without the fear of a commissar anywhere. He asked many questions and received answers, to which his replies were, "Interesting, I will have to think about that." After his release, he flew back home armed with a Bible and our addresses should he have more questions. Exactly a year later we received a short note from him (mailed from a harbor they had docked in). It read, "I have learned that 'man cannot live by bread alone.'" Bless the Lord for the working of His Spirit. We serve a faithful Savior!

I sincerely know that our brothers and sisters in Christ, both in the prayer group and those with whom we interacted, helped us grow for what was ahead of us in full-time ministry. Seeing the hunger for the word of God, on the one hand, and understanding that respondents to the gospel we were sharing may face persecution and even death, made a strong impression on my heart and life.

During these years all three of our daughters were born: Ilne in 1979, Mareli in 1981, and Hanri in 1982. They were close together in age and have remained best friends even though they now live great distances from one another.

# 3  THE NEXT STEP: CALLED INTO FULL-TIME MINISTRY

Ike, a full-time missionary with Brother Andrew's Open Doors Ministry, became a close friend during our volunteer years. Lida and I suspected nothing when he called to find out whether we would be home on a particular day as he was visiting our city and wanted to visit with us. We were surprised when he said, "We have need of a full-time development (resource raising) representative in this area (radius of 400 miles around Durban), and after praying about it we feel led to ask you to consider coming on board."

My world was in turmoil. I loved my job, but I was also serious about my commitment to walk out my faith. At the same time, I wanted to make sure that God knew that I was not applying for this job, so if I ever had to face imprisonment or worse, I could remind Him that the problem was not mine. Other questions loomed before me: our children were small, and this would take me away from home often. We had just sold our house and bought a new one (larger mortgage payments);

accepting the call would mean "walking by faith" (No income would be discussed until we answered the call). Moreover, I was an engineer with no experience in the field of public speaking or fund-raising. Could I be content without ships and the ocean?

When Ike called a week later for my answer, I could not affirm that God had given me a clear direction, but I undertook to spend the next day in prayer with an open schedule until I could reply to the call. Before sunrise, on that Saturday morning, I went to a secluded spot in our new house, which we had moved into during that week, and prayed, "Lord I will obey if you answer me so directly that I cannot mistake it for anything else." I wondered for a moment what that meant and imagined that I could not refuse if my name or the job description that Open Doors offered would be spelled out in some manner—how I did not know.

Immediately, I was drawn to read my scheduled devotion for that Saturday from the third Epistle of John. What I found in those 15 verses blew my mind. John and Johan are derived from the same root word, Johannes. He writes to Gaius (the correct spelling of my ancestral last name is Gaus) and the instructions to Gaius in verses 5 to 8 were an exact description of what my job at Open Doors would be: "Dear friend, you are being faithful to God when you care for the traveling teachers who pass through, even though they are strangers to you. They have told the church here of your loving friendship. Please continue providing for such teachers in a manner that pleases God. For they are traveling for the Lord, and they accept nothing from people who are not believers. So we ourselves should support them so that we can be their partners as they teach the truth" (NLT).

Apprehensive and out of breath, I walked back into the living room where I blurted out to Lida, "God has answered, and we are to accept the position with Open Doors, trusting only in God's provision from here on out." Her answer astounded me, "Yes, I know." On the second day after Ike had extended the call to us, God led her to read, "Leave your country, your relatives and your father's house and go to the land that I will show you" (Genesis 12:1 NLT). Her reason for not telling me earlier was that she did not want to influence me since I would be the one doing the job.

My resignation from the engineering firm had to be handed in before 9 am on Monday, the first working day of August, or I would have to work yet another month to provide notice. The resignation letter was in my jacket pocket when I arrived at the office. My boss and very close friend, Ian, was not in his office. I waited as my nerves frayed—I had already told Ike I would be available on September 1. Just before 9 a.m., Ian walked in from the boss's corner office calling me over to his own office.

"I need to speak to you also," I volunteered. As I walked into his office, he stopped, turned around and, extending his hand, congratulated me on being appointed head of the "de-gausing" division—a very highly specialized technical division that dealt with systems on military ships. I was shocked. There were only a few people in the country who even knew about this aspect of our work, let alone had the training to do it.

(I recognized the irony of the offer—a Gaus heading up the de-gausing division. I could imagine the jokes that could have come from that.)

I reached into my pocket and very quietly said, "I cannot accept the position because I am resigning today." It was a tense moment.

Ian turned on his heel and returned to the big boss's corner office. I was called in, and from the negotiations and offers it was clear they wanted me to stay. The offers were more than attractive, and I knew if I started considering them I would open myself to serious internal doubt and turmoil. The more I explained that "God had confirmed my appointment with Open Doors," the less they seemed to understand or accept my reasoning. Finally, they admonished me "to seriously think about it" because this was a really big deal.

^ ^ ^

*Lida's perspective: The Lord has always been faithful to give me specific Scripture when faced with a far-reaching decision. Looking back now after many years, I am encouraged to see that Genesis 12:1 came true again and again. The directive to move away from what was familiar, and even from family and friends, was prophetic for many years to come. In a sense we are still nomads, following obediently where the Lord sends or directs us, trusting Him.*

∨ ∨ ∨

God had the last word for me, and I finished up and left at the end of August.

So in September of 1982, the adventure you are about to read began. Today, 40-plus years from the time we stepped into part-time ministry, the following sums it all up: Not for one moment have I missed the ships, the ocean, or the excitement of seeing a ship that had taken 2 to 3 years to build, be launched, and commissioned. We enjoy going to the ocean on vacations. It has been a privilege to walk this path in the knowledge that our God is truthful, faithful and adequate. Those He calls He also anoints for the task He lays on them. Matthew 6:33 (KJV) sums it up well, "Seek ye first the Kingdom of God, and His righteousness; and all these things shall be added unto you."

Stepping into full-time ministry as a fundraiser presented a more-than-daunting challenge. A large number of our relatives and friends saw this move in a very negative light. Their comments caused us much distress. "You turned your back on a good, stable and well-paying career." "What were you thinking?" Or, "You have no theological training; how can you be a missionary?" "You gave up a great future to become a beggar?" "Living by *faith*, you have abdicated your responsibility to your wife and children. How are you going to provide for them at a level they deserve?"

Two people understood that my actions were not just personal choices but a step in obedience to the call of God, following the leading of the Holy Spirit. First, Lida never wavered. Her support just grew stronger as she labored to make it easier for me to travel away from home to speak at churches, banquettes, faith-promise dinners, businessmen's lunches, and wherever people would listen to the testimonies of what God was doing in countries where Christians were persecuted, jailed, and even killed for their faith. On average, fundraising meant being away from home for nearly 200 days per year.

My second strong supporter was my aging mother. Her prayers were the bulwark that allowed us to get through many difficult times. Often, we would find her sitting in her favorite chair with her hands folded in her lap, eyes closed, and lips moving as she interceded on our (and others') behalf. The enemy of our souls did not hold back during those early years, but somehow everything resolved for the good. Mom lived to the ripe age of 96 and never stopped "standing in the gap" for missionaries.

Our faithful God allowed me to see a miracle that grew my faith and allowed me to point to it every time I was asked about my hope or when I was in doubt:

Four of us traveled to Germany and hoped to go through Checkpoint Charlie (Berlin Wall). We applied to enter East Germany and, if possible, also Russia. Having South African passports, we realized that our chances were slim to non-existent, but we tried anyway. The lady took my passport, looked at it curiously (she had not seen a green passport before), read "South Africa." She turned and spoke into the office area, "Where is South Africa?" Without waiting for an answer, she stamped my visitor's Visa and proudly said, "Welcome." Upon inspection, she had given us Visas that would allow us to travel to Leningrad, Russia legally! Prayers answered in this way strengthened our faith in asking for it in the first place.

To be an effective witness about the persecution of Christians meant that we had to "strengthen what remains and is about to die" (Revelation 3:2 NIV). Brother Andrew often reminded us of this foundational call at Open Doors. A witness must have first-hand experiences to share (otherwise we're not "witnesses," we're just repeating hearsay). Thus, we traveled to:

Mozambique—The Communist government plunged into a long civil war where pastors were often targeted because they "controlled and influenced" people;

Malawi—where millions of refugees from the war in Mozambique sought refuge. Malawi did not have the resources to sustain such numbers and became the most impoverished country in the world for many years.

Angola—Just like Mozambique, it slipped into civil war after Portuguese rule was overthrown. Again, Christians were caught in the middle—not wanting to participate on either side, and therefore accused by both sides of supporting the opposition.

Ethiopia—There we did not need to ask evangelical pastors if they had been imprisoned; we just asked: "how long."

Zimbabwe: During the "liberation war" in Rhodesia (now Zimbabwe) we served Christian communities on many occasions and in many places. Christian farmers and mission stations were primary targets—for the terrorists they looked like soft targets. For us, they were the very objects of our calling.

Three God moments remain uppermost in my heart. I remember the dangerous situations into which we went to fulfill our calling to minister in Malawi, Zimbabwe, and Mozambique. Our call from God was our motivation for going:

**Malawi:** With the civil war raging in Mozambique, more than a million refugees crossed the border into Malawi. Already one of the poorest countries in Africa, President Banda had no other choice than to appeal to citizens to "take a refugee family into your home." This caused them to slide into even greater poverty. But by extending a friendly hand to the refugees, they showed the Christian love that Malawi, also called "the warm heart of Africa," was well known for. This paved the way for many of the refugees to receive Christ as their Savior. We sent good vegetable seeds to the church leaders who had participated in our leadership-development program. They distributed the seed to congregants who planted them and shared their produce with the refugees, who helped till the land and tend the gardens.

Neither of the opposing armies was paid, meaning they ravaged border villages where they found food by confiscating all they could carry. They accused villagers of colluding and therefore conducted these reprisal raids, "because you have been helping the opposition forces." Thus, Christians were caught in the middle and blamed by both sides. In some areas, it became necessary for Christians to move out of the villages into clusters of huts where they could support one another to stand against either of the armies who abducted able-bodied men to join them in fighting for their side.

Willie, a colleague from Open Doors, and I went into just such a situation. Our goal was to discover why so many raids had targeted churches in that area, as well as what we could do to alleviate some of their hardships. It turned out that churches were targeted because they kept a list of many members whom they controlled. The lists were considered a resource for recruitment and an excuse for accusing the pastor of "favoring enemies."

Near the end of our meeting with the pastor and elders of several congregations in that area, observers told us that a raiding party of soldiers had been spotted some miles away, and we should leave as soon as possible. We happily complied as we knew that our presence had not been detected—the soldiers had been spotted far off over a ridge and could not have seen us.

The following Sunday, in line with the safety arrangements the Christian village had made, they all walked to the church together. Two ladies were late and decided to walk to the church alone. What happened to them we do not know, but they were killed and laid next to the footpath to the huts. With the church service over the congregants started walking back home. They found the bodies and, in true African tradition, they surrounded the bodies, wailing and calling the families of the two ladies to come forward. As family members knelt down next to the bodies, they activated the landmines planted under them. The ensuing blast killed thirty-nine people. I will never know whether our presence had anything to do with that attack, but it surely weighs on my mind to the point that I am more than sensitive about exposing Christians who must remain in their communities while I can go safely away.

∧ ∧ ∧

*Lida's perspective: When Johan came back from that first trip to Malawi, something had changed in him, and it was visible immediately. The suffering he had witnessed and the forgiveness of the perpetrators was so unknown to us! But he also came back with an excitement of knowing the Lord kept them safe, and this experience could encourage others. He did not come back with a hero attitude; he came back in great humility and submission to the calling. Let me add that in my naïveté I had no idea beforehand where they were going—just as well.*

♥ ♥ ♥

**Zimbabwe:** During the "war to liberate Rhodesia," Willie and I were led to visit various places where Christians were under persecution by the occupying forces. We heard that the residents had come to believe that "the Christians had forgotten them." This thought stemmed from the many attacks on Christians with very little if any response from the outside world. The horrific massacre at Elim Mission on June 23, 1978, where all the missionaries at a mission station were killed, and even four toddlers were murdered, barely made the world news. There was no outcry from "the world."

Our colleague Mike, a resident Rhodesian, met us near the Rhodesian border with South Africa and introduced us to Claudette. She and her husband had started the Esther Movement, organizing local prayer groups to meet and pray specifically for peace and reconciliation in Rhodesia, which was later renamed Zimbabwe. The groups met at 6 a.m. every morning, and thousands participated and interceded for the war to come to a peaceful end. Claudette watched her husband gunned down. She and relatives who visited them for a braai (barbeque) successfully defended the house. After the incident, Claudette and the rest of her family moved to Salisbury (now Harare).

Mike informed us that Claudette would accompany us on our first trip into the southern province "battlefield" near the towns of Kezi, Plumtree, and Figtree. The farming community where Claudette lived earlier had invited us to minister at a Sunday church service. Both Willie and I were asked to share messages of encouragement for those who were weakening in their faith. As I stood in the pulpit, I noticed that there were more firearms than people in the church—each man over the age of 16 had a rifle lying in his lap and a pistol or two in holsters on his belt.

I cannot remember what Willie and I shared that day. I am very clear on what happened when Claudette was asked to speak to people who knew her family well. "I want to thank everyone who participated in the Esther Prayer groups. We are witnesses of answered prayers, where God intervened through miraculous events: Attacks were stopped, fear struck the hearts of attackers, causing them to flee. Attackers later said that they had seen images of angel forces at places they had planned to attack, prompting them to become believers, remembering that this was what they had heard as boys about Jesus. It was out of fear of God, not of the people, that they repented— again, answered prayers!"

Then she said, "I want to tell you a true story." In essence, this is what she told us:

"In a small town stood a church with a beautiful stained-glass window; tourists from all over the world came to marvel at the message depicted in it. But one day a violent storm blew the window out, and it shattered into a mass of broken glass. Nobody came to that church anymore. A master artist came to the curators of the church and asked about the whereabouts of the window. 'The shards are in boxes in the basement,' he was told. He asked if he could have the broken pieces. The elders agreed. A year later the artist returned and invited the elders to come and see what he had done. To their surprise, he had taken the pieces and rebuilt a window, more beautiful than the original, and it would fit in the place of the old window. After installing it, more people than ever came to view it.

"You all know how we all got together when we prayed in the Esther meetings. You also know what happened to our family when my husband was killed. I left the farm to live in the city. Well, I am here to tell you that the Master Builder, Jesus, has worked in my life so that I am going to take the gospel of Jesus Christ to the very men who fought against the Rhodesian army. I want to ask you to pray with and for me as I go."

There was not a dry eye in that little church that morning. We had all witnessed what true forgiveness was all about. As with the window, Claudette's life was reshaped to one of greater beauty and significance.

When I remember the impact Claudette's words had on all of us, I think of the crown she will wear in eternity for her commitment to Christ. "Do not judge others, and you will not be judged. Do not condemn others, or it will all come back against you. Forgive others, and you will be forgiven" (Luke 6:37 NLT).

**Mozambique:** One of my early mentors repeatedly admonished me to know that the enemy of our souls (Satan) would strike unrelenting blows when we were most vulnerable. In my case, this "baptism by fire" came with my very first sending out of a person on assignment. We needed to make direct contact with some church leaders in the central parts of Mozambique who had succeeded in sending a message about an alarming persecution of Christians. We needed to get one of our researchers to them to assess what their most pressing needs were and figure out how to get aid to them. The problem was that "Solomon" (not his real name for security reasons) was looking after his two young children, while his wife was in the hospital for the birth of their third child, a girl. The other person I could send, known as "Barnabas," was much older and not as well versed in protocols used in Mozambique. When Solomon heard that I was leaning towards sending Barnabas, he was adamant that he needed to go. I just needed to give him three days to arrange with an extended family member to "release him" from being at home.

I drove the four hours to meet with Solomon near the Mozambican border. After briefing him about the message we received and what we needed, we prayed together, and he left. Several days went by without hearing anything from Solomon. This was not unusual, but I found the pressure of facing "the unknown" growing, despite trusting God and praying with my staff for his safety.

When Barnabas called (I can share his real name, Baba Masinga, since he is now with the Lord), I was glad to hear that it was he, but I was not ready for the message. "Solomon has been captured and charged with treason because he had Christian literature with him." Bibles were considered contraband materials. Solomon made contact with a believer who brought food for a relative who was in the same prison and asked her to get a message to Baba Masinga. Because Masinga was so well known in Christian circles in Swaziland before the war, she knew how to get the message out—despite dangers to do so.

I was sick to my stomach when I heard the news because treason carried the death penalty if he were to be found guilty as charged, which we had no doubt he would be. (The term "Kangaroo Court" well describes the activities of the "army court" farce.)

We alerted our prayer warriors, and they sprang into action. I spent many nights on my face before God pleading for Solomon. I was the one who had sent him on the mission; his children were young; we could not make contact with him at all; he needed food and a blanket. (The state provided nothing for prisoners; the prisoners would get only what the family would provide.) Baba Masinga organized a network of acquaintances with the same messenger lady to take him the provisions we gathered. The most daring was when Solomon asked for a Bible. His message to us: "There are so many here who do not know Christ. I need a Bible to evangelize and show them that the words are not mine, but the words Jesus spoke."

Days turned to weeks, and still we received only sketchy information. Then came the next shock—Solomon was being transferred to the Mashava Prison—a death camp by many accounts. New arrangements were made to keep him fed and clothed. Again, a believer was found (not by "coincidence" I submit), and through relatives of the men who had stepped into a relationship with Jesus as Savior and Lord we received more information.

Before sunrise on the morning three months and 21 days after his capture, I was praying and asking God for his release. We knew this was not likely, but we drew great courage from the fact that he had been in Mashava for some time and had not been executed. In fact, the reports coming from him were more than just encouraging—he was seeing more prisoners rotate through Mashava than he would have seen in any other prison. We started to see God's hand move in this whole episode. I opened my Bible for my devotional reading, and there a verse jumped out at me: "I, even I, am he who comforts you. Who are you that you fear mere mortals, human beings who are but grass, that you forget the Lord your Maker, who stretches out the heavens and who lays the foundations of the earth, that you live in constant terror every day because of the wrath of the oppressor, who is bent on destruction? For where is the wrath of the oppressor? *The cowering prisoners will soon be set free; they will not die in their dungeon, nor will they lack bread*" (Isaiah 51:12-14 NIV, italics mine).

I jumped up and ran to Lida, not able to talk, pointing to the verses for her to read also. I had God's answer, and that was enough for me! When the staff met for our morning devotions at the office, I shared the Scriptures with them. We rejoiced and praised God for His faithfulness. Around noon my private phone rang, and as I answered it. All I heard was, "I am out." I recognized Solomon's voice immediately. The following morning after crossing the border out of Mozambique, he called me again and told me that he was fine and going to Baba Masinga's house. That was the fastest time I ever made it to Swaziland.

Solomon continued going into difficult places and situations representing Christ to the persecuted Christians. His mere presence and the "prayerful greetings" sent from the rest of our team—signifying that they were not forgotten—brought them great joy, which they expressed in worship to the Lord.

**4**

# TO JOHANNESBURG WE GO: FROM RESOURCE RAISING TO PROJECT TIMOTHY

**W**hen we were transferred to Open Doors' headquarters in Johannesburg, Ike, my immediate superior, and his wife Marietha continued investing in our careers and lives. They mentored us in word and example. During this time, we started understanding what was meant by the saying, "When God appoints, He anoints." Opportunities to raise funds for growing projects did not fall into our laps; we had to plan and organize speaking engagements where we could present challenges or opportunities for supporting projects. The success rate of organizing cold canvas by phone was somewhere around 3%; only three calls out of every 100 secured a speaking opportunity. Many times we faced seemingly impossible budgets; yet after bringing the figures before the Lord, the supply met the demand. This always brought times of celebration in honor of the God we served.

In just over three years of fundraising, we had many hilarious as well as some sad stories to tell potential donors. By God's grace, we were able to meet the growing budget every year, despite some rather dramatic growth phases in projects where needs multiplied as a result of increased persecution. Ike was the Director of Development for Open Doors for many years. It was delightful to work for him as our relationship went beyond friendship to being brothers. We rejoiced and wept together over many shared situations—persisting in prayer to discern God's will for implementing new strategic plans to meet nearly impossible budgets and times of doubt that we both had to work through: the death of my father; Lida's miscarriage; the births of all three of our daughters. Yes, interpersonal conflict (with others) happens even in ministry circles. Ike and Marietha were instrumental in guiding us to overcome them all by providing perspectives from Scripture that addressed our challenging situations.

Daniel, Program Division Director at Open doors, returned from Mozambique, burdened that churches were left leaderless by the onslaught from both armies. Pastors were imprisoned, killed or had fled for their lives. Daniel heard God's voice address the problem of leaderless churches in Mozambique, from 2 Timothy 2:2 (NIV): "And the things you have heard me say in the presence of many witnesses entrust to reliable people who will also be qualified to teach others."

Daniel, Peter (a Dutch missionary), and Ike worked on developing, evaluating and implementing what became known as Project Timothy. By the end of 1985, the basic program strategy was in place and seminars set up to which a group of leaders was brought to field test the program. Unexpectedly, Daniel announced he had received and accepted a call to lead in setting up a Christian school system in a very underserved area of Zululand. Neither Peter, who was returning to Holland, nor Ike, the Development Director, could add Daniel's Program Division to their portfolio. Thus, the position was open.

In January of 1986, I was installed as Director of Program Outreach, headquartered in Johannesburg. My job was to manage all the Open

Doors projects in six sub-Saharan African countries. Never in my life had I been more afraid of failing than right then. The "shoes" Daniel left behind were enormous. He was a giant in every facet of his being— spiritually, intellectually, organizationally, relationally, educationally and more. However, it soon became clear that the multitasking skills I learned in the shipbuilding world were my biggest asset. Working in many countries on different projects and with various leaders within those countries meant there was a host of moving parts to be managed. By God's grace, building on Daniel's well-laid plans, and with the steadying hand of Ike, the task became manageable. Humor characterized Ike's outlook on life—he was serious about his faith but could always find a reason for bringing levity into the execution of plans in challenging situations. His advice and support gave me the confidence I needed to follow through on God's promptings.

Addressing the most significant need of Mozambican churches— namely, a lack of trained leaders in rural village churches—would be a monumental task. Sticking to our calling from 2 Timothy 2:2, "… finding faithful men, … teaching them to teach others," was my guiding principle. It was at this point that the key to successfully train leaders in such remote locations became clear. It could only be done utilizing the principles of *mentoring* through people who spoke the local languages (at least 24 overall—of which 10 were major languages).

The most difficult questions had to do with logistics: How do we deploy Project Timothy in a country at war? Where and through whom do we present the training courses? How do we get the training materials translated into the local languages?

Implementing the program in the field was my baby. What was the best strategy to deliver quality training to people over long distances? Correspondence courses were not an option because of the low levels of literacy in the "bush" of Africa. Although we started in Mozambique, we knew that in all the countries we worked, sooner or later we would need to address this problem. Of the experts in higher education institutions that I approached for a resolution to my problem, most said it was not possible to reach our goals in the bush because of all the obstacles that mitigated against success. We had a dilemma: God had called, and now men said it could not be done! We could not resolve the problem through traditional Bible School models—students could not afford high tuition fees, most of the Bible schools are in the cities from where they drew their "qualified" students, and they were all full.

After many sleepless nights on our knees, a familiar model started crystallizing for us, a model which served me well in my earlier years as a student. The tutorials would operate out of a hub having these features:

**An apprenticeship structure** where teaching and the practical application of newly acquired knowledge would alternate.

**Classes conducted in the local tribal languages**, taught by a speaker of their language. For instance in Mozambique many people qualified to be tutors spoke Portuguese, the national language. We could provide the written materials in Portuguese in most places, while relying on the tutors to teach in the local dialect where required.

**A classroom setting.** Because the students were oral learners and literacy is low, face-to-face tutoring was needed.

**Within walking distance** of their homes. The trainees were not formally employed, as they eked out their livelihood by planting vegetables and corn on a small scale. So, they could attend any class within walking distance almost any day.

We realized then that the role of the tutor was the key to delivering quality instruction to church leaders (our students). He must be a *mentor* in the same way that our Lord Jesus walked and taught His disciples. Not only would the faithful man we identified teach the students, but he would also visit them during the week at their homes to discuss how they were doing in applying what they learned in class in their congregations. Further, he would attend meetings where he would observe the student as he led his congregation/community (and help if needed).

It was clear: Success or failure would rest squarely on our shoulders. Selecting the right tutor would be of cardinal importance. Where would we find him? In practical terms, we learned that this was not as difficult as first imagined. Foreign missionaries had done a great job bringing the gospel to the people (mostly in or near cities) and teaching church members. They just did a poor job of putting mature nationals into *ministry*. (The missionary's slogan remained, "I know how to do this; I'll show you.") Research in the field showed that there were outposts or preaching points set up by missionaries where they preached at least once in 3 to 6 months. Elders were appointed at such outposts. Although they were not allowed to "preach," they could retell the story the missionary shared until the missionary returned. The question I asked was, "Can faith be grown or sustained in this manner?" The answer is a resounding *no*.

We found these elders, deacons or whatever the missionaries called these outpost leaders, men who knew the Bible stories, and knew who Jesus was and what He has done for them. They already proved that they were faithful with little (by leading the small congregations in their villages for years), so we could help them do even more. In these faithful men, God showed us the final element in His plan to bring the gospel to rural communities in Africa—through local trusted leaders, within walking distance of the student's residences, in their own languages, with practical, culturally appropriate Bible-based curriculum. These chosen men already had a calling to be leaders in their communities; they just never before had the method of working in a multiplying ministry environment before. All that was required was for them to be equipped, empowered, and encouraged to fulfill the calling from God to serve their local communities and nearby villages with the gospel.

We started by appointing three chosen men, Elias, Leslie and Lucas (each from a different tribal background and language), to do the initial research and identify areas where Project Timothy could be deployed. All three worked with me for my entire 17-year tenure as Chief Executive of Timothy Training. Elias went to the Sotho; Lesley to the Nguni, and Lucas to the Tswana speakers—the three major language groupings from which most of the local dialects stem. These men could understand and speak many of the dialects in the areas where they worked.

Our strategy was simple: Each of these men, introduced as tutors, went into the villages where African Independent Churches (AIC) had congregations. These churches had broken away from the denominational churches over a century earlier and were very possessive of their independent status. Their leaders, in general, had very little, if any, theological training, yet they would have nothing to do with training emanating from mainline churches. We invited AIC leaders within walking distance of a suitable venue to a meeting where we shared our calling from 2 Timothy 2:2 and the desire to teach them strictly Bible principles (without denominational dogmas). Each tutor needed to ensure that the area they chose could attract 10 to 15 AIC leaders to the training program. This was not difficult, as there are thousands of AIC churches in rural Africa.

With the basic curriculum plotted out, tested, and adjusted to the culture, we could start moving. The next test for us was to pitch the training at the levels of understanding of our students. We accomplished this by using indigenous trainers who could adjust their teaching to suit the students.

Our initial goal was to enroll 100 pastoral students in the first year. Our trainers would mentor these students over a three-year period in three different hubs. Each hub would draw students from about 10 area villages, each within walking distance (three to eight miles). The tutor would offer classroom instruction to these 30 students three to four days in one week, and then visit the trainees during the next three weeks to see how they implemented in their congregations what they had learned. Some of the "graduates" would go on to train others, as they had been trained.

Find one Trained Tutor
Enroll 10 local church leaders who have
no training in each of 3 communities
=30 students.
Each tutor trains 30 pastors over 4 years.

Great was our surprise (and joy) when the enrollment numbers blew past 100 in only two months! The hunger for Bible training was so great that enrolled students spoke to relatives and friends, which resulted in each of our three tutors having multiple classes. We realized we needed to expand our volunteer teaching staff dramatically. To accomplish this, the tutors identified pastors who had Bible school training and who agreed to adhere to our rules for training AIC leaders. The benefit to them, receiving the instruction from an evangelism base, was that their own churches would grow, and their ministries would progress towards complete self-support.

My task was not only to manage the training program but also to find the funds to do so. By presenting the concept of using pastoral training as our evangelism model, I could access affluent churches more effectively. They allowed me to speak in Sunday services to their members with the goal of giving *them* an opportunity to fulfill the Great Commission by participating with *us* as we reached out to "the ends of the earth"—the bush of Africa.

Many established churches continue to do missions in the traditional manner: Sending their assessed missions dues to their headquarters. This removes close physical contact or direct interaction between church members and missionaries. It has been extremely detrimental to the interaction and relationships between supporters and missionaries. Missions thus becomes an activity between the denominational headquarters and people not known by church members personally.

Sending out missionaries who are from a foreign land (language, culture, style of living, and more) is expensive, and it takes years to overcome those barriers. Real spiritual fruit is only possible after a relationship of trust is established—something that can take years for foreigners.

But hearing from a missionary who had a multiplying evangelism plan to saturate communities with the gospel by empowering nationals who speak the local languages, understand the cultural pitfalls, and are trusted by the local community, made a lot of sense to the churches I approached. Add to that an invitation for them to participate personally in the program and to see how the return on their contribution/investment also multiplied, made for an instant hit. This was the primary reason, by God's grace, that allowed us to keep the expanding program funded.

These churches quickly began to sense the difference between these two scenarios: The average costs to prepare a family to go overseas (training, deputizing to raise support and to travel to the target country)—$200,000. Keeping the family on the field (house rent, vehicle purchase and maintenance, travel and operational funds)—$130,000 per year. Total expenses over four years—$720,000. I have no problem with spending God's money on God's work. However, when the results are examined, some reservations do occur. The missionary works hard at learning a language, getting to know locals well enough to invite them to his church, struggles and fails many times at culturally different approaches (which can set him back in making progress in the community). Then there are the two most significant factors: his influence (generously gauged) would be over less than 150 people, and the attrition rate for missionaries not returning to the same mission field after their first furlough is high. In some sending agencies, it could be as high as 50%. (These are average statistics obtained from sending agencies. Numbers differ from missionary to missionary and from agency to agency. This merely attempts to show the difference in cost basis between two models).

So investing $720,000 to influence 150 people is a low rate of return: $4,800 to evangelize one person before the first furlough.

On the other hand, by working with indigenous leaders for a similar period, the return on investment is multiplied. The average cost to support a tutor, the training materials, Bibles, transport for the tutor, and food (corn meal) for the days the students attend the three-day seminar comes to $300 per month. That amounts to $14,400 for a 48-month period (one year in organizing the hub, and then three years of actual training).

But an even more significant difference is found in the number of people in being trained (not just attending). Using an average of 20 trainees per tutor, 20 tutors x 20 students (on average) = 400 or $720 per disciple. To this, we add the cost of a Bible, graduation ceremony, diploma, and the price of a bicycle provided to the tutor for increasing his productivity in getting to his work. So, the total cost of producing a reproducing, disciple-making pastoral leader is around $940 per graduate. And not all the eggs are in one basket. At no time do you run the risk of losing one indispensable person around whom the entire ministry hinges.

I am not against traditional missions or missionaries; after all, I am one myself. I am merely pointing out that another option exists that is worthy of consideration. There are places where the traditional may be the only or best approach, such as places where indigenous Christians capable of being equipped are not available. But there are many places where national workers capable of being trained are abundant. I am advocating and presenting the case for expanding the workforce to include faithful indigenous Christians by equipping, empowering, and encouraging them to fully answer the call of God upon their lives, as well as allowing missionaries from sending countries. If God calls us, can he not also call them? When Jesus said, "Go ye…," there wasn't a single American or European present.

By the end of our fourth year we reached the long-term goal we set at the end of the first year: to graduate 500 pastoral students with a three-year Diploma in Ministry. We needed to revise our long-term goals. The fast growth and the resulting increase in personnel required to keep this as a project of Open Doors was becoming a concern in the minds of upper management. The staff (although mostly volunteers) was getting larger than that of Open Doors. Thus, when tutors and hub leaders arrived on Monday mornings at my office to submit reports of their week's classes and to get the training modules for the next week or two, space became a problem. A solution had to be found.

# 5    1989 TIMOTHY TRAINING INSTITUTE IS BORN

After much prayer and deliberation, the decision was made for Project Timothy to become a separately registered, non-profit training corporation that could issue tax-deductible receipts to donors. For me, this was a tough call. I loved both the covering Open Doors (as a successful International Ministry) offered on the one hand and what the envisaged Timothy Training Institute (TTI) represented on the other. Staying with Open Doors would be much less stressful, while starting anew with TTI meant building an entire organization from the ground up. It would be challenging to say the least. The fundraising aspects were my biggest concern—getting sponsors to change their donations from a trusted organization to a newly-registered group always presents major problems. What would the Lord have Lida and me do?

From Isiah 54:2 (ESV), we received our marching orders, "Enlarge the place of your tent, and let the curtains of your habitation be stretched out; do not hold back; lengthen the cords and strengthen your stakes." Once again, we were wholly inadequate in ourselves. We were on our knees before the Lord, trusting that He would open the new doors He set before us.

## Curriculum

We soon realized that the curriculum we wanted to implement was needed beyond the borders of South Africa. This meant it would have to be adapted further to accommodate the academic levels of our students. Adjustments were necessary.

This was a considerable obstacle, but again God had gone before us. Ike and I had met elderly missionary Pastor Fred Burke (originally from Springfield, Missouri) who had legendary status among many Africans, especially those who wanted Bible training but could not afford traditional Bible Schools. He had developed a curriculum that was available only as a correspondence course, thus excluding the thousands of leaders who could not read or adequately comprehend what was written. Remember, we had earlier concluded that, because Africans are *oral* learners, training would take place in contact classes, where a teacher could explain the materials in terms that would enable them to implement it directly in their congregations. Some of Pastor Burke's materials were already translated into tribal languages. We thought we would have to do that over time and appreciated this head start.

When we explained our vision (oral classroom training provided to pastors/leaders in their own language within walking distance of their homes), Pastor Burke agreed to let us use his curriculum as a transition to our own, which would be an adaption of his materials for our use in contact classes. This step was pivotal in the ongoing transition from Project Timothy to Timothy Training Institute.

What a legacy Pastor Burke brought to the table: At the youthful age of 17, he had left the shores of the U.S. to answer the call of God to go "to the ends of the earth" with the gospel. When Ike and I met him to negotiate the details of using his materials, he had served in Southern Africa for 65 years. At 82 he had the energy, stamina, and determination to "win Africa for Christ" that made most missionaries look like they were on vacation. At 90 he was still actively preaching at different churches where he was invited to bring the Word. He married again, for the third time, at 93. His "All Africa School of Theology" continues today, though he has since gone to be with the Lord.

Out of respect, Africans do not call someone more than ten years their senior by their first name. So I fondly addressed Pastor Burke as Uncle Fred. We had a very fruitful relationship for more than a decade. I was the real winner with all he taught me. As our work together neared completion, perhaps the most significant event in my life happened quite spontaneously.

I visited him at his home in 1995 to report how God was leading us to reach more and more communities in six African countries north of South Africa. With tears in his eyes, he got up from his chair, straightened up, took both my hands, and had me stand, also. He then laid his hands on my shoulders and said, "The mantle of my calling this day has passed from my shoulders to yours. May God bless and sustain you through your time in His ministry." I was humbled beyond words; I wept and had only an inkling of understanding of what had just happened or what it meant. He is one of the people I will be looking for when I join him in glory.

In addition to using Pastor Burke's training modules, we developed some of our own. Ike knew Reverend Vermaak, a retired pastor who ministered in the mission fields of Venda Land in northern South Africa. He was renowned for the stories he told to illustrate, in practical ways, difficult Bible concepts and passages. So we asked him about writing on some subjects we needed to address in our three-year curriculum.

Another spiritual giant in God's service, he agreed to help compose them. As he wrote, I had the privilege of previewing them. He had the capacity of letting Scripture declare Scripture by referring the students from one verse or concept to another where the meanings would (mostly) be self-evident. I learned more from Reverend Vermaak's writing than I can relate here. I very quickly realized that whenever he said, "You know what the meaning of this passage is?" I had to keep my mouth shut because I was going to hear (and learn) something I had never imagined.

I will never forget his story on pride. I visited him to pick up a manuscript he had finished and to pay him for the work he had done. He asked me to walk with him to his mailbox while he pointed out the damage done by a tornado that had touched down on his property— very old Cedar trees had been ripped out of the ground or twisted to look like corkscrews. He said, "I was walking down this way a week ago when I heard the Cedars talking to one another, boasting, 'I am glad we are so tall that we have this beautiful view over the valley. We can see all the way to the cliffs on the other side, unlike the lowly grass that cannot see beyond the next tuft obscuring each other's view.' The day after the storm I walked down here again to look at the damage. This time I heard the grass lamenting, 'Is it not so sad that the Cedars had grown so stiff that they could not bend in the wind?'" I knew I needed to take to heart the wisdom packed into those words if I wanted to remain obedient to God's call.

He overhauled our entire curriculum for us with such effective lessons that the materials were used by other ministries and translated into 18 different languages. He is another Saint I want to visit in glory.

One of the most impactful and transformative sermons he ever preached also was one with the fewest words used. He had accepted the call to a new congregation in an area where the majority of people living on the mountainside and the ridge were professional (white-collar) people, and those living on the flatland were blue-collar workers. This presented a unique challenge. The divide ran through the middle of the church as the two groups sat on opposite sides during services and had different priorities when it came to church council decisions. Previous Pastors had tried to bridge the divide and failed. Reverend Vermaak (his last name means "entertainment" if translated from our mother tongue) was very graphically descriptive in his sermons. He was also an accomplished trumpet player.

That morning his text was "equality before God." It took only a moment to tell the congregation that God's heart breaks over divisions and He desires unity in His Body, the church. He reached down, took his trumpet and played a piece of music on it. At the end of it he extracted the mouthpiece and inserted it into the spout of a (metal) watering can—and proceeded to play the very same melody. In closing, he pointed out that, in God's eyes it did not matter what we look like or what we do—our position in Jesus was equal brothers and sisters (children of the King).

One of the prominent doctors got up, walked over to a brother on the other side, hugged him and asked for forgiveness for some offense from years earlier. Then the floodgates opened as people were reconciled to God and their neighbors. The church was never the same. After coming to a repentant correction with itself, it grew in spiritual maturity and numbers as God blessed them

∧ ∧ ∧

*Lida's perspective: Johan grew up on a farm while I was a city girl. For many years he yearned for some open land around him, while I resisted. When we contemplated venturing into an Angora rabbit breeding and yarn production (hand spinning and plying) business, he became serious about moving out of the city limits onto a small farm. I still was reluctant, until the morning I sat down with the Lord and seriously laid the situation before Him. Despite my reluctance, I was ready to be obedient to His Word. Clearly, in my heart, I heard Him say, "Micah 4." Reading through this, the words that jumped out at me were in verse 10, NLT: "....for now you must leave this city to live in the open country." We lived on this small farm for 12 happy years in safety. Even though the property was not secured with high fences and gates, God had truly sent us there and kept us safe!*

❧ ❧ ❧

**6**

# GROWING INTO NEW OFFICES

By the time we moved into our new offices in 1994, the curriculum and translations were completed in a number of the major languages of countries around South Africa and Mozambique. We were ready to branch out more aggressively to Malawi, Zambia, and Zimbabwe. The staff grew as did the number of students and training modules, and so did our budget. Paying commercial printers for our training modules became our biggest single expense. It grew to the point that we decided to investigate doing our own printing. None of us knew anything about printing, so I called on Ike to help me research the best way forward. It was a blast. We laughed a lot at one another and ourselves as we navigated the world of technical terms and industry lingo we knew nothing about.

At our church, we found a small motorized ink duplicator, not unlike a mimeograph, that had been idle for many years. I took it out and checked to see whether it would run—it did. Next, we tested the "plate maker" to see if the lights worked. We knew that the paper plates were covered in wax and that the lights burned openings where the master document allowed the light through for the ink to get onto the paper as it passed through the machine. However, there was a "roller" lying on top of the machine that I could not find a place for. Thus, it was left out until I could ask a knowledgeable printer about it.

We bought plates and ink. By 9 p.m. that night the first papers with the text of our modules came off the duplicator. A few days later Ike and I went on an excursion to speak to a person who repaired printing machines. I took the "roller" with me and casually asked where he thought it fitted on that particular model of duplicator. Very dryly he said, "I believe that is the cylinder of a door closing mechanism." We were exposed as total novices, so he explained entire processes to us—from dampers and blankets to registration and grippers—and more.

By the time we walked into the next print shop they all thought we were "pro's" because we spoke in correct industry terms. When we told them that we needed to buy a printing press but had no idea what would serve our purpose, they thought we were joking. They were convinced we were in the printing business wanting to expand our shop. Over time they became close friends who served us well with all our printing machinery needs.

A friend from my days in Durban, Reverend Erich, had skills in typesetting. Those were the days before desktop publishing. I needed a person between the authors of the curriculum and the printing machines, and Erich came to mind. He was available, and our working relationship grew in depth as he ran the print shop for many years. Neither of us was a printer, but we soon learned how to run that in-house print shop to the point where we did not need to send any more work out. We printed all our training modules for much less than commercial printer rates.

I think The Enemy of Our Souls knows a lot about causing disruptions in printing processes. It became standard practice for us to stop all the machines in the shop when weird stuff went wrong with the printing press itself, lay hands on the machine, pray—asking for wisdom to know what the problem was—and gave praise to God for His mercy. Invariably, when we turned the press on again, it would run smoothly with no problems, *or* we would immediately see what was causing the problem. Remember this was long before a simple "reboot" could solve your problem.

My faith was stretched many times in that print shop, and we saw miracles happen when we were in dire situations. Through thick and thin, joy and frustration, we labored together for 17 years to provide each student the 30 training modules in the Pastoral Course. Without Erich's loyal support and tenacious hard work to get the curriculum done on time, we would not have had the successes we experienced.

One of the times where I was called on to stretch my faith came when Erich interceded for his nephew, Gerard. At that time we were teaching our students on how remarkable God's grace was—He paid for our sins while we were still His enemies (see the tool we use at the end of this chapter). So, how was I going to handle Erich's proposition to give Gerard, a dyslectic 20-year-old young man a chance at doing some work for us?

Some background information that had to be considered: Gerard did not finish his academic track at school, and he also dropped out of the technical training courses his parents arranged for him. However, he could strip and rebuild a car engine with no problem. Erich asked me whether Gerard could repair the engine of an old delivery van that had broken down. I needed a vehicle in the print shop, so I agreed to a price for the job. In no time and under budget we had our vehicle restored. Was there anything else I would allow him to do?

I testify to God's favor that will always be with me, in what happened to this young man who suffered from severe dyslexia. We took a chance with him, just as God took a chance with us by offering His only Son in our place.

A tantalizing option was to have him assist Mr. Bellamy, our fully qualified printer, who was aging and whose health was deteriorating. The problem was that if he got hurt, I would be in for the high jump. When told that he was not to do anything on any of the machines other than prepare and load the heavy paper stacks into the hoppers of the machines, he jumped at it. The two of them became inseparable.

In time Gerard told us that Mr. Bellamy was having trouble with some of the adjustments to set the machines up fully; could he help since he had carefully watched how it was done? I agreed that he would be allowed to do the set-up jobs that Mr. Bellamy directed him to undertake and that Erich would be responsible for overseeing the speed of his learning curve. The assistance Gerard provided fitted the description of an apprentice, but we were not a registered entity that could train apprentices towards becoming artisans.

With the introduction of much improved, high-speed office duplicators and Mr. Bellamy's retirement, we decided to change the print shop from a commercial venture (accepting outside printing jobs) to an in-house duplicating operation printing only our own manuals. Erich spoke to a brother in Christ who worked at a large newspaper company, and Gerard was accepted as an apprentice. He distinguished himself as a printing machine mechanic and has since been sent all over the world to repair printing machines.

Every time Gerard and his family speaks to either Erich or me, he expresses his thankfulness to God for having been allowed to have a chance in life. He used it well, and they are a productive family in their community, serving God.

As redeemed children of God, do we—or would we—take the risk of offering someone (a neighbor, perhaps) a chance at an improved life if it were in our power to do so? That's what our course is all about.

Recently, I was invited to speak at a little church where Erich is helping out in his retirement. What a privilege to stand with him and share God's Word reflecting on nearly 40 years of brotherhood.

Because Erich was our point man on printing our training manuals, our major budget item, he also intimately partnered in praying for the revenue. At times we needed to print, but the budget could not sustain the payment immediately, and we would confer, pray, and step out in faith for the funds to come in by the time the invoices for paper and ink fell due. We were also determined not to use the "the check is in the mail" line for fear of dishonoring the Lord's name—we would rather speak directly to our supplier to explain our dilemma. About two weeks after I had explained our dilemma to a supplier, he called and said, "I am coming past your office this afternoon, can I come and get the check?" My reply was that he could come, and we could enjoy a cup of coffee together. I knew this would take some hard negotiating for more time because it was a significant amount.

However, I grabbed my car keys and asked Tina, my administrative assistant, to go to the mailbox to get whatever mail had come in. She came back with only a few envelopes. I opened them all, except one. I concluded, from the shaky handwriting that it would be from an older AIC leader enquiring where he could go to enroll in the training—on the back was written, "To God be the Glory." There were a few small checks in the mail, nothing that could make a difference to my anxiety for meeting my visitor.

I gave Tina the little envelope, leaving her to send the relevant information out. She came back into my office, held the envelope out, and said, "I think you should look at the content." It contained a check for the exact amount we needed to pay the supplier. I dated the check to the supplier for three days later to allow the funds to enter our account. He was happy to receive it, especially when he heard the testimony of what had happened.

I need to stress two points here: The check had no markings that would allow us to identify the donor, so he or she remains anonymous to this day; that little envelope arrived four more times in the 17 years while I was CEO of Timothy Training Institute. I never failed to recognize it again! And each time it arrived when we had serious needs. To God be the glory for the things He has done! For both Erich and me, this remains one of the miracles that shows God's faithfulness.

As an example of an Evangelism tool in the curriculum depicting the methods used to equip the Leaders to reach the people who have lower levels of literacy, I include this Chart with its descriptions. (These teaching aids have been developed for Africa where Africans live intimately with these animals and consequently understand their behaviors. Africans learn visually, making such tools invaluable for evangelizing.)

## THE HEART OF MAN

We share the gospel through the presentation of four hearts of man. Heart 1 is the top image.

**Heart 1—We are born with a fallen nature into a corrupt world.**

**The double throne:** In the center of the heart sits Satan, the ruler of this fallen world, and *me* with a fallen nature in a fallen world. I hold the shield and spear to protect "myself," since I at least know Satan cannot be trusted.

**Animals:** The animals depicted here represent the characteristics of sins that bind us—rendering us unable to break free from the "kingdom of darkness."

**Peacock:** Pride. The easiest time to catch a peacock is when it is strutting proudly displaying its beautiful tail feathers. At such a time you can come up quietly behind the peacock and easily catch him. In the same way, when we pridefully boast, we can be unaware that Satan already has a firm grip on us.

**Since monkeys** like to chatter, they represent gossip, loose talk, propagating unfounded stories that demean and diminish our neighbor.

**Snake** has a forked tongue that distinguishes it from a worm. Scripture commands us that truth and lies should not come out of the same mouth. Can sweet and bitter water come from the same spring?

**Hog:** No matter how clean you scrub a pig, when he is released he will return to wallow in the mud. In the same way, we may be "cleansed" in our religious practices, and yet tell stories and jokes that do not belong in the mouth of a child of God. We also do not turn off undesirable and contaminating programming on TV. We do not walk away from unsavory conversations (or stop them). Contamination breeds further hurdles in our lives.

**Chameleon** can move its eyes independently. Many times, we are on the prowl to gain from someone else's misfortune, e.g., frivolous lawsuits or gaining the upper hand through unfair means.

**Crocodile** is the master of camouflage: He lies very still below the surface of the water with only the two dots of his nostrils breaking the water surface so that he can breathe. Unsuspecting animals coming to drink are easily caught because of the stealth of the crocodile. How often do we revel in "gotcha" moments that harm neighbors?

**Dog:** Infidelity. That "scent" sends all the males into a frenzy—many see infidelity as "the new normal."

**Frog:** As a coldblooded reptile, its body temperature corresponds to its environment. Many people will let their conversation and behavior slip to the temperature of their company or environment, failing to maintain godly standards.

**Lion** demands power, dominance. He must be boss, even a self-centered dictator. He bullies others to promote his self-supremacy. "I deserve it" is the enemy of humility.

**Mouse** hides behind inability, fear, and an attitude of "I am worthless," "I have no talents," "I am useless." Often it is a false and exaggerated humility and timidity.

Not everyone has all these sins in their lives, but all of us can identify the reality, and the dangers of the situations described. In some cultures, some animal characteristics are interpreted differently, and some may be offended by these descriptions. So some materials differ to accommodate local culture.

## Heart 2 (at the bottom)—A heart subjected to self-willed, personal effort.

Notice the great "Me" on the throne. Self-centered choices and decisions leave us responsible for the consequences they bring, even if we have heard the gospel but have not surrendered our hearts to trust in God.

The cross only depicts that I have heard some gospel-truth and have decided to attempt to do better, but I'm relying on my own efforts.

Some of the "animals" are partly driven out or gone for some time, but they can return and display their characteristics. We cannot overcome or be released from the compelling desires to sin by our efforts. The more we allow outside influences to feed these desires, the less victory we have over them. "Do not be misled: Bad company corrupts good character" (1 Cor. 15:33 NIV).

**Heart 3 (on left)—The True King is on the throne.**

Only when Christ assumes Kingship and sits on the thrones of our lives as our King and Savior are the holds of sin broken in our lives. Only when people are reborn into the new Life of Christ can their lives please God and bear fruit that is to His glory. That is when they begin to live under the direction of the Holy Spirit. The dove represents the indwelling of the Holy Spirit and the book, the Word of God. Reading, praying and submitting to the guidance of the Holy Spirit now characterizes the believer's life in the Kingdom of God.

The bunches of grapes and leaves represent our growth in walking with Christ and the bearing of the fruit of the Spirit (Galatians 5:22-23).

**At this point, Jesus sits alone on the throne of the heart and rules supreme while our lives are in submission to Him.**

**Heart 4 (on right)—Crossroads**

We tell our trainees, now that this information has been presented to you, you have two roads to choose from: Choosing the wide road means you love the world and want to go with the crowd and its godless pleasures. It culminates in disaster and eternal condemnation.

The narrow road limits your worldly activities and leads to eternal Life in the Kingdom of God, in whose presence there is joy.

We ask them: Do you understand what Jesus Christ has done for you? His sacrificial death on the cross paid for *all* your sins and has now taken you from being lost in sin to having the eternal Life that only Jesus Christ can give by reconciling us to God.

Do you believe that He can set you free from your sinful life? Do you want to *trust* and sincerely *follow* Him?

**Then we pray:** Father in the name of Jesus I come to ask for your forgiveness because I realize that I have been living under my own rules and command. I ask that you take control of my life and use me in your kingdom for your glory. Please lead and guide me to be sensitive to your voice and obedient to do your will.

# SOME EXCEPTIONALLY FAITHFUL MEN

I n relating so many inspirational stories it may sound like our lives and ministry had plain sailing. While we are happy to tell about the blessings of God, we also had some difficult times that tested our faith. Out of them came some cherished moments that will not be forgotten.

## Baba Masinga

Reverend Edward Masinga was a giant in Christ. His capacity to recall Scripture verses applicable to almost any situation that people get into continued to amaze me. He was the Senior Tutor at Timothy Training Institute. His stature within TTI soon grew to the point that everybody referred to him as Baba Masinga (mentioned in chapter three).

Baba, in our African culture, means a person of high honor and respect, a father, mentor. And that is what he became to me, my spiritual growth mentor. His family home was in Swaziland, but he taught classes as far away as Cape Town (near the Southern tip of Africa) and Mussina (on the northern border with Zimbabwe). In both those places, as in others, we needed a man who could deliver the gospel message with authority born out of deep trust and conviction of salvation wrought by Christ Jesus our Lord. His skills as a tutor were unparalleled in TTI. As my mentor, we spent quite a lot of time together in a discipling relationship.

Later in life, when he was about 75 years old, diabetes took its toll on him. Neuropathy made his feet hurt so badly that he would sit to teach. Whenever any rumors surfaced that he might retire, his students would plead for him to "just finish our class"—they knew their privilege in having him as their tutor. It was at the beginning of his suffering from diabetes that he asked me to visit them at their home in Swaziland the next time I would travel in that direction.

They welcomed me with great excitement. I did not know that he had called his entire family to be there on that day. At the lunch table, he said that the family had a request for me, "Would I consider being their (cultural) son?" A higher honor could not be bestowed upon someone like me (a white South African) by a part of the Royal Family of Swaziland. At the same time, I realized this honor had some strings attached to it. One of them was that I would be called upon at the time of his death to officiate at the burial ceremony and participate in the cost of the funeral (amongst other duties as a son).

I was able to fulfill my privileged obligation to bury him in a cool sunrise ceremony on a Friday morning on the hill behind his farmhouse (traditional family land) in Swaziland in 1997. God met my grief and request for His words to comfort the more than 1,000 people at his funeral by sharing our hope from Ps. 116:15 (ESV), "Precious in the sight of the LORD is the death of one of His saints." A majestic Cedar fell that day from my life.

^ ^ ^

*Lida's Perspective: Baba Masinga and his dear wife Annie stayed with us every time they had to travel through Johannesburg. The impact their relationship had on me was profound. Annie respected and served Baba with so much love, while he cherished her with a sweetness that is not common in many marriage relationships in Africa. They lived what the Word says about "submitting one to another." It opened my eyes to such a relationship and created a hunger to live like that.*

∨ ∨ ∨

## Antonio

Antonio lived in Maputo and was the country coordinator for Mozambique, overseeing the training of leaders in that war-ravaged country. He was always ready to laugh, had a flashing bright smile and a work ethic that was inspiring. I soon learned that his open and soft-spoken approach to life was not a weakness but indeed a strength. His ability to plan and execute the plans with precision endeared him to me as the head of the ministry.

I often combined reasons for meetings, graduation ceremonies, curriculum delivery, and quality control trips to make sure I remained in close contact with the people on the ground whom we were called to serve. Crossing borders in Africa is quite different to crossing them in Europe and America. As you enter a country, the driving rules, physical money, and the local languages change. Border posts can be a nightmare. Following the instructions while filling out forms in an unknown language, making the correct declarations of what you have in your vehicle without giving rise to unnecessary fees and searches can be daunting.

On such a trip, I decided to drive the truck scheduled to deliver Bibles and study materials myself. I dutifully filled out the customs forms and did everything the way I understood to be required. The last step was to give the Gate Guard the stamped documents which would allow the boom to be lifted and I would be on my way. But no, he told me to open the canopy door on my truck, he feigned surprise at the boxes of books and triumphantly declared that I was not truthful when I declared the training materials as "of no commercial value—not for resale." He contended that I was going to sell the manuals and would, therefore, be liable for import duty. He wanted me to pay him the assessed amount instead of having to go stand in the lines again, and he "could not leave his duties at the gate to go with me to the customs office." He made me pull off to the side so that other vehicles could pass as he opened the boom for them.

I explained that we had written the books, translated them, printed them, and I was now delivering them to give them to our students, *all free of charge*. No go. He explained that he gets paid from the customs collected at that office and as such if I did not pay duties and fees he is working for *free*. Of course he wanted a bribe, and I was not going to give one. This "contest" went on for about three hours. Frustrated, an idea occurred to me to ask him whether he smoked. He did, so I asked him for his lighter which he handed to me. I took two boxes of books out of the truck and set the box flaps on fire. As I reached in to put a third box on the two already there, he protested loudly. "You are not allowed to make a fire on Government property." "I am not taking them back to my office," I replied, "and I am not paying a bribe, so I will burn them here if you will not let me pass." He could not get the boom open quickly enough, and I nearly could not get the flames put out without using a fire extinguisher. No books were damaged, only the outsides of the boxes were scorched. When I told Antonio of my encounter, he laughed saying that he had difficulties with this same guy many times when he brought books back after coming to my office.

Some years later, in February of 2000, a cyclone (a hurricane in the southern hemisphere and spinning in the opposite direction) caused enormous amounts of rain to fall on the higher elevations of the plateau well inland from coastal Mozambique. The runoff coming down the mountains flooded the extensive flatlands. It was more devastating because the flood waters came overnight to a place that had not seen a lot of rain. During the rescue efforts undertaken by the South African Defense Force, helicopters, boats, and heavy vehicles were used to reach people marooned in trees and on high ground, cut off from the outside. Someone in a helicopter filmed one of the extraordinary stories of that time: a young woman had climbed into a tree and delivered her baby just before the helicopter swooped in and plucked them from the tree. The video footage was shown on many newscasts.

Many mud huts were washed away, and thousands of people lost all they owned. Many waded out or were rescued with only the clothes on their backs. Among them were four hundred of our students.

A considerable effort was launched to help our brothers and sisters, and God blessed our efforts. We raised enough funds to buy all the kitchen utensils, sleeping mats, clothes, cornmeal and vegetable seeds for each of the families to restart their lives. A Christian businessman (friend of our ministry) provided us his 30-ton truck to haul all these supplies and 400 sets of training modules. Antonio with his pickup truck and I with mine did the final distribution of materials to our students.

It was on one of the very last of these delivery trips to an outlying area that Antonio and another evangelist were stopped, and the vehicle hijacked. Antonio and his companion were both shot in the incident, and neither survived. To this day the loss of my friend and colleague (as with some of the others spoken of in this book) remains painful and begs the question, "How can I make sense of their untimely deaths outside of the sovereignty of God? I can only trust Him and obey Him in the knowledge that He does not make mistakes," as I do. God's answer to my desperate call came when He revealed His heart about His children in Isaiah 57:1-2 (NLT):

> Good people pass away;
> the godly often die before their time.
> But no one seems to care or wonder why.
> No one seems to understand
> that God is protecting them from the evil to come.
> For those who follow godly paths
> will rest in peace when they die.

I trust this is of comfort and value to you if or when you ask the question, "Why so young?" or "Why someone so talented and effective in reaching people with the gospel?"

## Phillip

When one of our key trainers brought Phillip to apply to become the tutor in a very volatile area south of Johannesburg, I was not positive about his chances of being successful:

> He was too young (culture does not look kindly on younger people teaching their elders);
> He was very soft-spoken and seemed almost timid—not something that I thought would stand him in good stead as a teacher with authority; and
> He was a Xhosa while Sebokeng (where we needed a tutor) was predominantly a Sotho-speaking area.

As the interview progressed, Phillip grew in stature before me. He spoke eight languages fluently (including Sotho). The way he answered questions from the five senior trainers and me showed that he was wise beyond his 25 years. Not only did he apply scriptural principles deftly to the problem posed to him, he also answered cultural nuances that the much older men struggled with (work-based acceptance; ancestral worship; bigamy; inter-tribal squabbles, and more). He was also able to help solve problems we were facing with the translation of materials because of his language skills. The final straw that convinced me he would be a great asset to us was that he was a strategic planner. When the final vote came, it was a loud and unanimous "yes" from all.

Working with Phillip was delightful. He would accept any challenge, anywhere, and return with the job done well and bearing fruit—his goal for all he did. I remember visiting a class in Sebokeng where most of the students were bishops, not just local pastors, denoting that they were the top leaders of their African Independent Denominations. Qualified leadership (from Titus and 1 Timothy 3) was the subject. Some of the older men had more than one wife, so the question arose as to their positions in leadership because Scripture requires that "a leader (elder) must be a man of one wife," 1 Tim 3:2 (ESV).

The debate very quickly excluded the way that the foreign missionaries had done it—forcing the bishop to send all wives, except one, away. This was one of the reasons their paths diverted from the mainline denominations more than a century earlier.

So, what was the answer? The students tried to defer the question to Phillip and me, "What is the teaching of TTI?" they asked. Phillip remained resolute; "You have to come to the answer so that *you* own it and implement it." (TTI policy did not provide glib answers but got the students to wrestle with the problem posed, under the guiding hand of the tutor. That way the students who participated in arriving at the answer owned it.)

After more deliberation, one of the oldest men (who had not said a word before) cleared his throat and said, "To me, it is like I am walking in the veld where I step on a thorn that breaks off in my foot. I have a choice; I can continue walking and feel the pain at every step, or I can sit down and remove the thorn." With that, he sat down, and there was an awkward silence. I asked, "Bishop, can you help us by telling us what your parable means?" The wisdom of his answer was profound, "We know now what the Bible says. I must make a choice. If I remain as I am, knowing that I am disobedient to the God I am wanting to serve faithfully, I would lose my peace through disobedience. No, I must make an agreement with my two younger wives that I will look after them and our children and remain as the husband of only my first wife. Or I can give the leadership of my church to a man in my church who has only one wife. I will remain as the founder of this church, but I will appoint him as bishop, and he must lead the whole church from now. This is what I decided." Over the months following, Phillip was able to guide nearly all of those students to choose one of those solutions. Today both of those choices are proposed in our materials. In more recent times fewer men have more than one wife, but it still happens from time to time.

As the winter of 1999 approached, Phillip got a cold that he could not shake. Later he came down with pneumonia. His symptoms became more frequent, and we sent him for extensive tests. Nothing showed up for a while. Then he undertook a long trip with a very crammed schedule, and when he did not arrive back home on time, I became worried. When he did come, he said he was exhausted and that he had a strange growth of blood on his upper lip.

It turned out that he had contracted AIDS at his initiation ceremony. Entering manhood, young Xhosa men are sent out into the wilderness for a month to survive on their own, eating plants, roots, berries, and leaves. All part of showing that their parents taught them what was edible. When they return, they are circumcised. The traditional method of circumcision is still practiced: the "knife" is the sharp edge of a stone and the "anvil" a flat stone used as the cutting board. Neither is cleaned between procedures. There is a lot of blood at that point without good hygiene. We learned that some of Phillip's contemporaries had also contracted this monstrous disease. His condition deteriorated, so I had his family move into an apartment on TTI property (about two miles from my home) to be able to "walk the road with him." By then, we had become close brothers.

On a Saturday, the young man who worked in our print shop came running to me and shouted, "Do you know what is going on at the apartment?" I did not. "Some relatives arrived with a *Sangoma* (witchdoctor) to curse the people who invoked the curse on him and to cleanse his body by making him drink *muti*." (Muti is "medicine" the witchdoctor has concocted.) Immediately I was in my car.

I am not sure whether they had seen my car coming, or why they left, but when I ran into the apartment, only Phillip's mother, wife and two boys were there. Phillip was exhausted. "Phillip, can you tell me what happened here earlier?" I asked. "No," he replied, "there was a lot of noise, but I was too tired to understand or respond." When I mentioned that a witch doctor had been there to "do his magic," he was oblivious to what was done and had not participated. At this point, he seemed to fall asleep. We learned later he had slipped into a coma. I concluded that he was in the coma while the witchdoctor was doing his thing.

I walked back to my office and called Erich, told him what had happened, and asked him to come down so that we could pray over Phillip. Erich suggested waiting until morning as he was non-responsive at that time. I knelt at my desk and asked the Lord to give me one more time to speak directly to Phillip.

"He's awake," our printer said from the door. I called Erich again and asked him to come as fast as he could. We went into the apartment, and I asked Phillip whether he could tell me whom he could see. He named us all. I asked him to pray with us, and he answered that he could not, he was too tired. We prayed around our little circle. As I concluded my prayer asking for protection from what had taken place that afternoon, he responded, he said "yes" and sighed. His head, which I was holding in both my hands turned slightly; my friend had died quietly at the age of 29. Praise our Lord, He answered our prayers, giving us the opportunity to stand in the gap for Phillip.

I drove the vehicle carrying his body to his family property and buried him. There I greeted another hero in faith with whom I had the privilege of rubbing shoulders. Although I do not want to second-guess God, I did wonder (and still do) why someone like Phillip, with so much potential and love for his Lord, was extracted from the battlefield at such a young age. Peace and contentment came in these words, "There are 'friends' who destroy each other, but a real friend sticks closer than a brother" (Proverbs 18:24 NLT).

## Witchdoctors and AIDS

A few notes on Sangoma's and AIDS are prudent here.

Unless one has seen and experienced the reality of curses and demonic forces at work, it is difficult to comprehend what can happen: objects or people can fly through the air and slam into walls to show the demon's power. Someone may ask a witch doctor to place a curse on a person they don't like or consider an enemy. The victim will then become ill for no apparent reason—and no physical medicine will be effective. Sometimes a man's voice will come out of a female victim. The demon may cause the victim to start growling like an animal and attack the person the family brought in to help him or her. The demon doesn't want to give up its occupied home.

Another time we were asked to come and pray for a young pregnant woman whose abdomen convulsed so badly it looked like she would burst. Her jealous rival had asked the witchdoctor to place a curse on her unborn baby. When the demon was rebuked, it left with an unearthly scream. The woman became calm and later gave birth to a little boy. Although premature, after being in an incubator for several days, he was fine.

It is not uncommon for people who have been cursed to die within a short time of being cursed by the *Sangomas*. The Bible is not silent about the powers of darkness, as in the attack on the sons of Sceva (Acts 19:14-16) and Satan presenting himself to Eve (Genesis 3).

Yes, people with AIDS are among church members in Africa. If there were none, we would not have done our job. People who come to repentance and into a relationship with Christ after being sinners for a long time receive forgiveness of those sins, but the consequences of sin do not necessarily go away. This is where Christian love blossoms most beautifully and compassion allows us to serve them without condemnation, despite the dangers of infection.

Two major ways in which AIDS spreads rapidly in the African context are:

- Truckers infected with AIDS infect prostitutes at truck stops. Then successive truckers become infected from the prostitutes. The women also infect any local partners
- Migrant workers, of whom there are multiple thousands in the gold mines of South Africa, find alternate partners while away from their traditional homes for long periods of time. They infect these partners or vice versa. On returning home, they infect their wives. The Christian message of abstinence has been fairly successful in breaking this practice.

Although other ways exist, they are not as fast-moving as the above. For example, Philip was infected at an initiation ceremony that eventually caused his entire family to die. However horrible that was, it at least stopped there. In the most rural areas where no medical help is available, whole families in villages are similarly lost. Our work at one stage was severely affected when we found it difficult to get pastors together on Saturdays because of the numbers of funerals that were being conducted.

The son of a pastor friend contracted the virus through receiving infected blood during a transfusion. When he was diagnosed positive to AIDS, he and his wife decided that they would not have children, since by then she had been infected, also.

These are some of the demons we contend with as we preach the gospel in Africa.

**8**

# GOD PROFOUNDLY USES YOUNG PEOPLE

F ollowing one of my daughter's performances with the Youth
Orchestra, an accident left a young violin player, Stephan, seriously
injured. He lost three fingers from his left hand when a device
used to simulate the canons in the "1812 Overture" malfunctioned
and exploded. Since I was going on a mission trip to Malawi and he
was recuperating at home, I suggested to his parents that he come with
me on the very long trip. I had no idea the significance his presence
would have.

The trip took us through Zimbabwe. I had previously set up a
meeting with some missionaries who worked in the area near Kariba
Lake, but I did not know how to get to them. I stopped at a gas station
to ask for directions. The gentleman gave me precise details—he knew
the missionaries I was going to visit. He made clear that we needed to be
very careful at one point when we would be driving alongside the fence
of a banana farm. Many elephants came there to eat the spoiled bananas

and vegetables put out for them to eat. That part of the road went very well since we knew of the potential for trouble.

Further down the road we rounded a bend in the road and saw a sight stranger than I had ever seen. Two trees had so many vultures sitting in them that I stopped to get a photograph. Stephan opened the door and pointed his camera at the trees over the top of the car. We debated what the vultures had seen and why they would be up in the trees and not on the ground. We agreed that there had to be a dead animal nearby. We got out of the car and walked over to the other side of the road, thinking we would be able to see what was happening down in the deep ditch next to the road.

The Elephant grass was eight feet tall, so we walked forward blindly, parting the grass directly in front of us as we went. Suddenly the grass opened to a clearing, and I could see three lions at their kill. They had heard the noise we were making and started backing up and circling—not a good sign. I screamed, "Lions!" and scrambled up the embankment as fast as I could. Fortunately, my door was on the closer side of the car. Stephan had a bit longer way to run than I. Our doors slammed as one, and we laughed at each other, speculating what it may have looked like to someone who may have been watching these two dummies who should have known better.

Recently on a trip to Ireland, I saw a sign at a pub where we had lunch that reminded us of our folly: "To be old and wise you must have been young and stupid before." We should have remembered it, at least, for the rest of that trip—but sadly we did not.

Some days later, Stephan and I were driving through Gaza province in Mozambique on our way back from Malawi. A "policeman" stepped into the road and flagged me to stop—not unusual per sè. Rolling my window down a bit, I greeted him in my best, very limited Portuguese. Quick as a flash, his hand went straight for my car keys, and he pulled a pistol from his jacket pocket. "Money!" he barked. My thoughts were racing as I told him to calm down. His hand was shaking so badly that I thought he might fire the pistol involuntarily. My young companion, Stephan, took his wallet out and the gunman went around to his side of the car. That gave me the opportunity to get out of the car, pull the cash I had from my hip pocket to throw it under the seat of the car out of sight, but if you have ever tried to throw folded bills, you would know that they do not fly well. So the money unfolded, hit the seat, and lay there in open view. He took all our money, demanded more, and did not accept that we had so little cash on us. Stephan, who worked at a gun shop during school vacations quietly said to me, in our language, "That gun cannot fire, the magazine does not fit properly." My reply was, "Are you sure? What if there is a round in the chamber?"

At this point, the thief told me to open the trunk and empty the contents of our suitcases onto the road. He was looking for more money. He had my car keys and all our money and was holding us at gunpoint. Suddenly, a thought shot through my mind: *Hit him!* But he was out of arm's reach. To get him to come closer I blurted out, "I need some of my money back because I need to put gas in my car!" Even the thief responded to this African necessity. He stepped forward as he peeled a bill from the roll in his hand and threw it at me. The same thing happened to the money that had happened when I tried to throw it under the seat—it fell to the ground.

He made the mistake I was waiting for: he watched the money fall to the ground. I took one quick step forward, and my fist exploded on the side of his face sending him into a cartwheel, causing him to drop both my car keys and the gun. Stephan's injured hand precluded him from any aggressive action, and the thief landed too far away from me to grab him and pin him to the ground (I am heavy enough to do that). He rushed away with all our money, except for the bill he had thrown down.

Back in the car, Stephan asked, "What are we going to do now?" "Pray," I said, "for God, who knows our dilemma, to cover us in His grace and to be our constant companion as we drive to the Zimbabwean border—and, since you asked, please start us off in prayer." We used the bill (equivalent to about $12) to put gas in the car along the way. The last 200 miles the gas tank gauge needle lay on "E" (Enough, in God's economy). When we turned into the driveway of a friend where we could get help, the car stalled without gas—we had traveled 530 miles on just over a half a tank of gas! This is the God I heard Brother Andrew talk of, who again answered the prayers of His children.

**Youthful Evangelist**

In the execution of our Strategic Plan to meet people where they were, we had to be innovative in developing materials for evangelism, to help people walk with Jesus as their new Savior and Lord, and to help grow new believers to maturity in their faith. We use different materials as we address varying situations. The picture flip charts (double legal size paper) were particularly popular when working with children and non-readers. Fifty-four full-color pictures show a Bible story on each page, equally representing the Old and New Testaments. A pocket version, depicting principles for our lives for each of the stories, also was produced for leaders who attended the teaching sessions. Making spiritual tenets understandable in their experiential world helped them grow phenomenally and become witnesses of Christ.

Mary, a 7-year-old daughter of a pastor who attended the training seminars, lapped up every word her father said when teaching groups. She got to know the stories and their applications by heart—not unusual in an oral learning environment.

Wherever you go in Africa, there are tons of kids. So, whenever Mary shared the stories using her dad's pictures, many children crowded around to hear the messages contained in the pictures. When I was privileged to go to that area again some two years later, I was asked if I would like to visit Mary on Sunday before the church service. (Adults often see the acts of children as inferior and not worthy of too much attention by adults.) I accepted the invitation. When we got to the schoolyard I was stunned; I could not take in what I saw. Mary had a Sunday school of over 200 children who had learned the way of salvation from her and who were now professing children of God.

Right there I experienced the full truth of God's word, "Assuredly, I say to you, whoever does not receive the kingdom of God as a little child will by no means enter it" (Mark 10:15 NKJV).

Sadly, I never saw her again. When I returned two years later the drought had dispersed families all over the country to wherever they could find a way of eking out a living, usually along rivers or streams. Nobody knew where they had gone.

**9**

# REINFORCEMENTS —
# COOPERATION AGREEMENTS

fter speaking about "Multiplying Leadership Development" at a conference in Johannesburg, leaders from two independent ministries approached me to ask whether they could use our curriculum in their programs: Evangelical Rural Mission and Harvesters International Ministries.

## Evangelical Rural Mission

Dewald, founder and CEO of Evangelical Rural Mission (ERM), had previously been a South African Special Forces officer in the Angolan war. He had come to faith in Christ and received a call to go and serve the people he had earlier fought against. This nearly proved to be disastrous. He was well known in the Angolan border region, and when he was first recognized, he was captured by the opposition forces who were still clearing the area in the aftermath of the war. By God's grace, he was released and went on to minister in another area for several years. He also needed training materials to train some leaders he had assembled in central Mozambique, and our ministries worked together there for over 30 years. As ERM grew, we also ministered together in Malawi, Republic of Congo (Brazzaville), Mozambique and Namibia.

Wherever you go in Africa, there are always people walking and many children. So the ministry expanded to include outreach to children/orphans (under the supervision of the pastors-in-training), forming the Children Harvest program. Dewald's crew introduced the highly successful concept of commissioning mothers and men and trained them to be storytellers.

They shared Bible stories with the children one day a week after school. Since there were so many child refugees/orphans left to fend for themselves, the Children Harvest clubs impacted their lives deeply. In some places, the children were allowed to sleep in church buildings (often only clay walls with a thatched roof) to have some protection against the elements. Most of them were orphans from war-related causes; as time went on, orphans from AIDS-related causes also were served.

Widows are amongst the most vulnerable people in African tribal society. The relatives of the man, especially brothers, are seen as the closest family to the deceased and so are entitled to his possessions—even the fields his widow worked with her husband to eke out their living. The brother sometimes might choose to take the widow as a wife. In cases where the husband had AIDS, the disease would then spread further.

Often, however, the widow was left without any support system, leaving her to beg or dumpster-dive for scraps to eat. To address this problem, we partnered with a local church to supply vegetable seeds and gardening equipment to widows so they could produce food for themselves. We then placed three to five orphans of the same sex in her care, and the local pastor helped motivate the children to help her weed, water and pick the produce. In this way, orphans were cared for, and the widows became positive, productive members of society again.

The Provincial Governor visited a meeting of residents at the ERM mission station in Gondola, Mozambique, and asked one of the widows what she could share about her work with the orphans assigned to her. Her answer was significant: "Caring for the orphans by providing our food and not begging, my dignity in society has been restored. People do not see me as a burden anymore." Thus, our Dignity Project was born. Proverbs 31:25 describes such a woman: "She is clothed with strength and dignity, and she laughs without fear of the future" (NLT).

Assigning children of one sex to a house mother (widow) helps prevent teenage pregnancies. African children become sexually active at a young age due to poverty and tradition. The family lives in a small hut without ceilings or separating walls, and the intimate actions between husband and wife cannot be kept private. Keeping the children of one gender per home helps prevent premature teen experimentation with sex.

The Dignity Project continues in many other locations, benefiting many widows and orphans. Some of the grown children have even enrolled in the pastoral training program.

### Pygmy outreach

In a long and fruitful relationship with Dewald and ERM, another milestone was reached when Dewald announced that God had burdened his heart for the Pygmy people in the rainforest area of the Republic of Congo, the second largest rainforest after that of the Amazon.

Several Pygmy tribes live in the harsh conditions of the forest. The air is very hot and humid, laden with pollen, spores, and mold, and every kind of stinging/biting insect. Also, Pygmy colonies roam around in the forest (always within their tribal boundaries). They are naturally very superstitious and leery of foreigners and strangers, and there are rumors that some of the tribes still practice cannibalism. They believe that every death in their camp is caused by curses or spiritual forces. They fear the power of the witchdoctor and break camp and move after every death. The chief is seen to have the most potent medicine and therefore is considered the conquering sorcerer.

In preparation for his first trip into the forest and in hopes of providing some security for Dewald, a Bantu man named Roffin was sent to find a Pygmy trader, who bartered with the Bantu living around the forest. The Pygmy trade meat they hunt for salt, sugar, cloth for their loincloths, and other commodities. Roffin took a photo of the "White Missionary" that he could show the chief if he could get to him. He hoped he would be able to try to secure an invitation for Dewald to come and introduce the gospel to the tribe.

Roffin found a Pygmy man from the Babongo tribe and asked to be taken to the chief when he returned to camp. Chief Moketo left Roffin waiting for seven days before allowing him to present his case. The photo caused a huge reaction because none of them had ever seen a white man. Chief Moketo then let Roffin wait for another two days before giving his permission for Dewald to visit them.

Upon arrival at Chief Moketo 's camp some months later, Dewald and Roffin were again made to wait for a couple of days. Presenting the gospel in an atmosphere rife with sorcery, witchdoctor activity, demonic manifestations, prejudice against the "unknown," and the acute accompanying fear of reprisal from their gods was not easy. We believe that only the cloud of intercessors praying for the missionaries shielded them from harm.

It also provided the breakthrough. A small baby was brought to Dewald—the skin on his head was a mass of pus oozing from insect bites that had turned septic. Everybody in the tribe knew that death was the only outcome. The mother had even run away into the forest, believing that death was the result of a curse. Thus, a relative brought the child to Dewald.

"You should not touch the baby," Roffin told Dewald. "If you touch him and he dies, or take him into your arms, and he dies, they will blame you."

Undaunted and following the prompting of the Holy Spirit, Dewald donned gloves, took out a tube of ointment, and spread it over the infected areas. He then fashioned a cap from bandages so that the little fellow (and others) could not scratch or touch his head with hands that were not clean. The instruction was that the baby had to be brought back on the third day.

To the surprise of most, he survived, and when the cap was removed, the entire infection had cleared; no signs of the infection remained. Nearly the entire camp came to see the result of the missionary's power. Was it strong enough to overcome the fear of the demons that plagued them? Amid gasps of wonder, the Pygmies wanted to name the baby "Dewald," but at his insistence not to do so, they settled on naming him Baby David.

Having experienced this victory, they were now ready to listen to the presentation of Jesus as Savior and Lord God (not a god). The first to respond to the message of salvation and receive forgiveness of his sin was Chief Moketo himself. His wife followed him. Over the next days of instruction in what all this means, those who had committed their lives to following Jesus changed: levels of fear receded, prejudices were cast off, superstitions were overcome, and evidence of an optimistic joy started to appear. At this point, Chief Moketo instructed his son to lead Dewald and Roffin to the other Babongo camps with the message that they must listen to the gospel told by the missionaries. In this manner, Jesus was introduced to the tribe.

When Dewald completed his circuit and returned to Chief Moketo's camp, he learned that the chief and his wife went to pray every morning before sunrise. Intrigued, he told Roffin to go and listen to what they were praying. Before dawn he found them sitting quietly. After a while, Roffin asked them what they were praying. Their answer showed us how careful we need to be when working with people who have no Bible or church knowledge. "We cannot pray ourselves; we are waiting for you missionaries to come and pray when you get here. We are just waiting for God to look into our hearts." What openness they displayed.

Dewald had to leave, but he developed a five-year plan to evangelize all the Babongo Pygmy communities. When he returned a year later, other Pygmy tribes had heard good reports about the Babongos and also welcomed Dewald. The carefully worked out five-year plan to reach the Pygmies was completed in one year. Before Chief Moketo died, we had helped construct a church shelter in his village, an answer to his prayers. God's timing in this instance confounded our logic for what would be required. He is sovereign, and we need to remember that.

We learned another lesson when we entered the domain of the enemy unknowingly.

After erecting the small church building at Chief Moketo's, we were asked to construct another at a village where the congregation had grown rapidly. The local elders had designated a piece of land for the building. Soon after the builders started digging the foundations, they complained that they could not sleep in their tents because of strange noises in the night (glass breaking, howls of animals, footsteps outside the tents). Not too much attention was given to it by the on-site overseers until some of the workers walked off the job. The overseers made arrangements to sleep nearer to the village, and the problem subsided—for a while.

Then, when the truck delivering the building equipment and materials drove up the hill, weird things started happening. The driver attests that the truck jerked, lost power and the engine cut out. Nothing like that had happened before. No matter what he tried, the brakes had no effect. The truck gained momentum as it rolled backward. Without the power steering, the driver lost control. The truck rolled over, killing three of the workers who sat on the back.

Paul, ERM's Congolese project coordinator for the building, rushed to investigate what had happened. When he arrived, he selected to sleep on the new church site. That night he was attacked, and in the darkness found it impossible to see who was fighting him, or from where the next blows would come. He fled through the bushes, with a broken arm and a multitude of lacerations. While the attack went on, he also heard the noises reported earlier. Later he went to the village where he was told that this particular piece of land had been used as a training area for witches and that the witches from the surrounding area had celebrated "victory" through the previous two days.

None of the original laborers were prepared to return, so new ones had to be recruited. Local pastors heard of the tragedy and arrived to use spiritual warfare to expel the dark forces and proclaim Christ's dominion over the land. The foundations were anointed with oil, the building prayed over, and the workers committed to God's protection before the work was resumed. The construction was completed, and the congregation continued to grow.

Following the exploration to find the Pygmy tribes, Dewald turned his attention to the furthest reaches of the Congo rainforest—places that can be reached only by boat. He planned to go from one fishing village to the next on the three major rivers running for more than 1,200 miles along the Congo border. Doing so, he would reach not only the Pygmies but the many Bantu tribes living near the rivers. So Dewald and Paul (his Congolese project coordinator who had replaced Roffin) set out on a rubber Zodiac with a 40 h.p. outboard motor. In three months' time, they shared the gospel in fishing communities all along the three rivers. On subsequent trips, we saw a lot of spiritual fruit as a result of their pioneering work.

Many people had migrated to the river towns to find work. There they heard about Jesus but lacked insight into the Scriptures. These were sought out and mentored towards a mature faith. Learning that ERM-trained pastors would be able to mentor them on a regular basis helped get them to commit to a consistent walk with Christ. They began sharing the gospel, as well, and many more souls came to repentance and salvation. Thus, that first exploratory trip produced not only immediate results, it continued to multiply results in succeeding years—all because we obediently followed Christ.

Together, Dewald and I had many more experiences, both positive and negative, but we knew that God had given us His grace and the privilege of going to "the uttermost part of the earth," knowing that He was with us even to the end.

My takeaway from all the times Dewald "disappeared" into the forest was the relief each time he "appeared" after being in places where we had no contact with him for weeks at a time, not even knowing if he was still alive. Twice we did have serious scares, but after each of those occasions, we *knew* that God was in control.

One time, stepping into the boat, Dewald fell, dislocating his shoulder. He suffered for three days before they could get him to a person who could reset the shoulder.

Another time an insect laid its eggs in his tear duct. When the eggs hatched, the larvae bored into his eye. They found a doctor at a logging station who had the correct medication to treat the eye. No ill effects remained in the long term.

As Dewald diversified the places he went—into areas no one else would ever think of going—God used him mightily. This ex-Special Forces officer, indeed, had had a profound encounter with the Savior. He answered God's call as a pioneer missionary to take the gospel into uttermost part of the world—even to places where Hope Builders

Ministries (the US based charitable organization, incorporated in Virginia in 2001, to advocate on behalf of partner ministries in Africa) did not have a calling or the resources to go. It was like trying to manage the whirlwind.

Reverend David, who had worked with ERM for many years, accepted the mantle of further developing the Hope Builders Ministries (HBM) profile in Southern Africa. He stepped up to seek leaders who could deploy our training programs in central and southern Mozambique (where he had some contacts from his earlier ministry work), Malawi, Zimbabwe and the south-eastern parts of Zambia. You will meet him again when the Disciple-Maker Program is discussed in chapter 14.

## Harvesters International Ministries

After I finished speaking at the conference in Johannesburg, several people were waiting to talk further about our training model before I even got to my chair. I had spoken about the exponential multiplier effect locked up in 2 Timothy 2:2 extended to the fourth generation from Paul to Timothy to faithful men and then to others.

Steven, founder and president of Harvesters International Ministries (HIM), began by saying he needed to talk to me about using our materials in HIM's Hub Model. He very briefly laid out the principal elements of the Hub Model and the reason for his interest in a cooperative agreement. What he sketched more than captured my attention. We set a meeting for two days later where we would both have an opportunity to explore how and what benefits both ministries could derive from close cooperation, or if there were any factors that kept us from entering into an agreement.

Find or train one tutor. The tutor picks
ten men from churchless villages.

Each student finds one village in which to plant a
church for each of the three years he is in training.
This will produce 30 church plants in three years.
Thus one pastor/tutor can produce 40 pastors over
seven years. (10 original + their 30 disciples).

## HUB MODEL

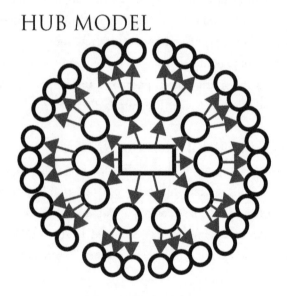

HIM was rapidly planting churches in several African countries but was hamstrung by not having access to a curriculum pitched at the level of the leaders they wanted to train to supply the churches with pastors. The main problem was that they could not find fully trained pastors to lead prospective church-plants. In turn, our model for training pastoral leaders in African Independent Churches worked well, but we needed to find more congregations needing pastoral leaders. It looked like each of us answered the other person's prayer.

Fairly early in the meeting, we concluded that this was a divine appointment—the visions and methods of working complemented one another like a hand in a glove. We worked out the details about giving

HIM the use of Timothy Training Institute curriculum, and HIM giving us the rights to use their Hub Model.

The training classes would be conducted after working hours for three hours on five week-nights. For those who were available during the day, we could do three days per month. Classes would be within walking distance of the students and conducted in their tribal (heart) language. Each class of ten would complete the diploma course in three years. The tutor would work a maximum of three weeks for evening classes, or nine days per month when they had three class groups running concurrently.

Our cooperation with HIM introduced our curriculum to different local languages in Zambia, the focus of HIM's outreach. That pressured us to translate our materials into four more African languages. There are 72 tribal languages in Zambia. We focused on the four major languages. Most Africans speak five or six languages, and usually at least one is a major language. So if we translated into the four major languages, we could reach Zambia.

Over the next decade through many ups and downs, we saw God change many leaders, churches, and communities into His witnesses, for His glory. Through the years, we shared much in our walk with the Lord; we also had many laughs. One stands out above all the others in its scope, impact, and absurdity: After a full day of doing presentations of our work at churches in Charlotte, N.C. we started looking for a hotel. We had no idea that the next day was "race day" and race fans jammed the city. All the affordable accommodations were full, and the ones where space was available we could not afford.

Finally, we drove a bit farther out of town. Through some trees, I saw a building with "...tel" on the blue facia board, so I turned in that direction and found a Motel. Steven saw some vehicles parked near the back fence of the property and commented that they must have been there for a long time, pointing out that there was grass growing right through them. Even so, Steven insisted I go check out the condition of the room, while he remained in the van. All seemed in order, so I checked us in. The rate was quite low, and maybe that should have given me a clue about the motel, but I was oblivious to it.

Steven was a big man, and I immensely enjoyed seeing the "ripples" run down his body when he "jumped" at fright—and he could react very sharply to a surprise. He grabbed the room key from me, opened the door, sat down, and turned on the TV. He expected me to carry all our suitcases and equipment into the room. With his attention focused on the TV, it was easy to catch him off guard and see him jump when I made an unexpected noise. I did it straight off the bat on that occasion. When I brought the last equipment into the room, he was not sitting there. Then I heard him calling from the bathroom, "the toilet is blocked."

I called the front desk, the handyman was not on premises, but they could give me "a plunger pump" to use. Well, because I was not the one going to use it, I agreed to come and fetch it from the reception desk. I was met with "Sorry, I cannot find it" when I got there. My simple reply was, "Then give us another room." This meant packing everything up, driving to the other side of the motel and unloading again. By this time, I was sweating heavily since it was a hot, muggy day. I needed to get some ice to get cold water to drink. The ice machine was across the parking lot, so with the ice tub in hand I walked over there. I was determined to "get" Steven upon my return.

Approaching the room, I wondered why he had closed the door as I had left it slightly ajar when I turned the air conditioner on to expel the hot air from the room. This gave me another advantage because he could not see me coming. I slammed the door with my shoulder and burst into the room, expelling my entire breath in the loudest roar I could muster. Strangely, from the bed a man shot bolt upright and there was a woman beside him. I was in the wrong room! I knew he could not chase me, so I jumped out and entered our room hastily, two doors over. Steven jumped at my fast entry, but I was not laughing at him this time. I just told him to "shut up." I didn't want that guy to hear any voices from our room—he was a big guy.

After telling Steven what had happened he very dryly said, "You realize that you were the angel of light today." He expressed that theory, surmising what the score was. Moments later, two cars pulled out from in front of that other room.

The relationship with HIM was extremely fruitful: thousands of churches were planted, and pastors were trained for each one of them. After about ten years of partnering, HIM grew so much that we mutually decided the time had come for them to embark on setting up their own resource-raising team. They accomplished that successfully.

### Growth at home base

Besides working in partnership with several independent ministries, our own ministry activities grew. This meant that new functions could no longer be accomplished by volunteers and new staff had to be employed. More office space was needed, and printing facilities expanded. This was the biggest step I had to take in faith because the growth exerted pressure for expansion but the revenue sources were stretched to their limits. Now, it was my time to P.U.S.H. (Pray Until Something Happens) and happen it did.

A former colleague from Open Doors was returning to Holland and indirectly had an influence on the sale of a small farm within 5 miles of the offices we occupied. The large old farmhouse was more than adequate for what we needed. During the negotiations to set the final terms for TTI to buy the property, it was clear that God's hand was moving. The bank approved our loan application even though we had never owned any property and our credit rating militated against approval. The seller was willing to donate a tithe on the sale to TTI, and our monthly mortgage payment was equal to the office rent we were paying in town.

Encouraged by the faithfulness of the Lord, we were ready to take on the next challenge. As the student numbers of TTI increased, so did the budget. Not able to find enough sponsors in South Africa for the rapidly growing training program, I realized that I would have to research ways of going on trips to raise resources in either England or America. I sat in my office praying one night after hours, and it grew dark. I desperately called out to God for a resolution to the increasing squeeze on our funds—either we had to get more funds or stop (or at least curtail) the growth in student numbers. I knew how hungry the students were to learn from God's Word as well as the subsequent hunger for spiritual food within their congregations. More funds would have to be found.

When I finished praying, I turned the lights on to straighten my desk when my eye fell on an American missions magazine a friend had given me. As I flipped through it I saw an article criticizing a previously published letter titled "Thank you for *not* going," advocating partnering with nationals in ministry. TTI was working exclusively with and through national Christians (no foreign missionaries in any of our teams.) Though I did not agree with the new article, I thought the original one was spot on.

Using the magnifying glass from the print shop, I could read the telephone number on a small image of the letter the advocate for partnering with nationals was holding (which the current author was criticizing). The author of the original article was Dr. Bob Finley, president of Christian Aid Mission (CAM) in Charlottesville, Virginia. My prayer then changed to asking God to give me favor with him when I called. The line was as clear as a bell, and when I asked to speak to Dr. Finley, I was patched straight through. After introducing myself and our ministry vision, he invited me to their facilities to organize trips to speak in churches and with groups who would listen to our presentation.

Within six months I made the trip to Charlottesville. It was a hard slog to get appointments set up, but I had contact with a supporting foundation. They introduced me to three other foundations who asked that I submit grant proposals. Within months after that trip we received enough funds designated for the production of our curriculum. We could grow sufficiently to accommodate applying students. I made deputation trips to the U.S. annually, and this very fruitful relationship lasted ten years. Again, God had answered our desperate prayers with outcomes far beyond our dreams.

# ^^^ 10     SHORT-TERM OUTREACHES

O ver the years many people on short-term mission trips have seen and experienced outreach in Africa. With Africans being very hungry for the Word of God, great outreach partnerships have developed. Missions to us means active proclamation of the gospel message through evangelism or discipleship. So even though we acknowledge that church-to-church ministry, such as digging wells, painting houses, building structures, is useful, we object to those funds coming from the "missions" budget. For us, missions trips are the vehicle where we focus on two goals:

- Local believers: Train members of the local congregation (with the pastor's supervision) in the how-to of one-on-one evangelism. Sharpen mentoring skills for growing relationships with Christ and fellow men in discipleship, and

- Team members: Increase confidence in the visitors to practice in their home churches and communities what they have learned and taught on the trip. We have observed that deep changes take place in the lives of both locals and visitors as they experience God working in their hearts and lives, as well as through them to others.

Pastor Bert's congregation in Michigan stands out. Over 50% of his church members went on mission trips to Africa. As preparation for their mission trips, his members would go on a weekend training/orientation campout in tents, come rain or shine, in less hospitable areas of Michigan. The biggest team he brought to Zambia consisted of 19 church members. Many times, God helped us overcome obstacles beyond our control.

The connecting flight from Michigan to JFK Airport where I was to meet them was delayed. If they didn't make it in time, I would have to rebook passengers on a route where the planes, generally speaking, are filled to capacity. I groaned at the thought. Then just as the final boarding call was made I saw "Big Bert" running up with his crew—they made it!

But boarding the plane was only the first obstacle. A power outage in the control tower delayed our flight for more than two hours, causing us to miss our evening flight from Johannesburg to Lusaka, Zambia. At Johannesburg airport, I tried to get the team rebooked. But smaller planes flew the later route, and there were not enough seats open. I appealed to the operations manager of the airline. After listening and doing some checking on a computer, he made the mistake of asking me what I would do if I were in his position. I answered, "That would not be hard to solve, just assign a bigger aircraft to this one flight." He pushed his chair back, picked up his telephone and spoke to someone and said, "We'll see what we can do for your group on tomorrow morning's flight."

Now we had a new problem: how to provide overnighting for 20 people in the airport building. I called Pienaar, a close friend, and he called another. Both of them lived near the airport and had vans. They took us to their homes where we got to sleep on the couch, floor, and wherever, more comfortably than in the airport. And by the time we arrived, Pienaar's wife had made soup and sandwiches for the entire team. My guests were floored.

Astounded, Pastor Bert asked, "How could you call them after 9 p.m. and in the winter, and ask for them to receive us?" "This is Africa," I said simply. "Friends help where they can when asked."

Our hosts took us back to the airport in good time for me to visit the Operations office to hear whether we were on the flight. "Yes, a bigger plane was available, and you are on it." But we weren't off the ground, yet.

It had snowed overnight (a rare event in the dry atmosphere in Johannesburg), and the freezing temperatures had turned the moisture on the wings to ice. Of course, they had no de-icing equipment, so we sat in the aircraft waiting for the sun to thaw the ice. Nearly three hours later, we took off for Lusaka, Zambia.

For the village outreaches, the group of 20 was divided into ten groups of two. Each pair was introduced to the ten local church members who enrolled beforehand for one-on-one evangelism training. The pastor of the participating church plus a translator completed each outreach team. We fanned out over the area around the town of Mazabuka, Southern Province of Zambia.

On Monday we trained the locals in the use of the evangelism materials we brought with us. After that, we took to the streets to speak to people or to knock on doors. Every evening we would debrief by asking the teams to share the highlights of that day. As the teams swung into action, excitement began to build. As they shared the gospel message, they saw lives change as they responded.

We showed the "Jesus Film" every night at a different venue; thousands came out to see it. They were especially fascinated that Jesus spoke Tonga, their native language. Many picked up rocks and threw them at the screen during the crucifixion scenes to show their opposition.

During that week, we recorded the names of over 2,000 people who made a profession of faith. Each name was given to the pastor of the local participating churches so that follow-up could be done immediately through them and their newly trained squad of evangelists.

Hands-on activity changes lives on both sides of the ocean. People who take such trips return equipped, empowered and encouraged. Our goal is to mobilize all the participants, African and American, to continue evangelizing and making disciples when they return to their homes and churches.

Through all the years of working with Pastor Bert, our bond has grown stronger. He now pastors a church in Tennessee and is urging his members to go on mission trips as part of their faith-growing experience.

### A very holy communion

Schnetler, a pastor in a large denominational church on the south coast of South Africa, and Nora had become very close friends of our family in our time with Open Doors. They, with us, believed avidly in empowering indigenous leaders to reach their own people. So he invited me to speak at his congregation on a number of occasions. They lived in a beachfront home to which they invited missionaries to "retreat" from time to time. During those respites, while relaxing and overlooking the Indian Ocean, we spent times in significant conversations about our ministries, deepening our relationship. Taking a short-term missions trip together cemented the bond between us thoroughly.

I was on my way to study the impact our training was having in an impoverished area of Malawi—a very safe place to take visitors. So a small group of five, including Schnetler and his wife, Nora, accompanied me.

Driving between two meetings, we came upon a road accident that had just happened (dust was still hanging in the air). A pick-up truck carrying bags of corn to be milled into cornmeal had rolled over. Two men were sitting on the back with two more in the cab. The driver and his inside passenger were shaken up but not injured. The others were not so lucky—one had a head injury but was coherent, just bleeding profusely; the other was ejected but not quite far enough to escape the edge of the rolling truck which came down on his leg and all but severed it above the ankle. Nora, a nurse practitioner, automatically went into action. She folded a piece of clothing and gave instructions on how to apply pressure to the head wound without causing more damage (we had no idea whether the skull had fractured), while she gave her attention to the man with the leg wound. "Is there a hospital nearby?" she enquired. Our colleague driving our van answered that there was a clinic not too far away. While applying a tourniquet to the leg, she said, "He is going to bleed out unless we get him to medical help."

I reorganized our team and equipment in our van so that one of the injured could lie on the floor and the other on a seat. What I did not know was that Schnetler was very squeamish when it comes to blood. When I saw him hanging out of the side window as far as he could go "for fresh air," I was reminded of the portion in Scripture that says we are all part of the same body but that each had a different function. Schnetler would have been useless to stop the bleeding on either of those patients.

God showed the group how He could use each one of His children in an emergency. Our responsibility is to discern our position in the body and what role we are called to play, and to be ready to play it to the full. (About six months later I got a message from our colleague. He told us he had received a note from the clinic. In it the man, whom I was sure had lost his foot, wrote thanking us for helping—his foot had been saved, and he was learning to walk in physical therapy classes).

We traveled on to the next stop. Though we were hours late, our African brothers and sisters were waiting for us, singing. I am always amazed at the ability (and grace) of Africans to sit down and sing, praising God while waiting for visitors to arrive. Although the sun shone brightly outside, the interior of the little mud-walled, thatch-roofed church was fairly dark. As soon as we sat down, after being introduced to the pastors who had come quite some distance, we were handed our welcoming gift. Each of us received a small, glass bottle of Coke and a brown paper packet containing three crackers.

If you think this was a silly refreshment, you don't know the significance. The host church leaders did not have cash to buy the treat they intended to give the visitors. So, they all chipped in a couple of eggs, or a couple of sticks of sugar cane, or some vegetables, or whatever they could trade, for money. One of the elders then took the cash and set off to buy the gift. He walked for three days to get to a shop to buy the Cokes, but had only enough to buy one packet of crackers. He asked for the paper and carried them back to the village where they repacked the crackers into the brown paper portions. But it became something even more significant.

Holding the elements in my hands, I explained to the visitors what this represented—they were giving the best they possibly could. Then a novel idea shot through my mind. I leaned over and asked Schnetler whether he would be comfortable to serve communion with these elements to the Brothers and Sisters if they would agree to it. He consented, and they replied that they could not remember when they had last partaken of the Lord's Supper.

In a language other than his mother tongue, Schnetler brought a short message and served communion to the 35 pastors and visitors present. At one point I heard his voice crack (and so did my heart), knowing what this meant in the lives of these brothers and sisters. The joy and worship emanating from that group after the meeting was beyond inspiring. For many years, until Schnetler's passing, we would not greet one another with the normal, "How are you?" but with, "Do you still remember?" That memory will go with me to glory. But it meant even more to those pastors.

A long while later I received a package. When I opened it, I saw the gift of love. In commemoration of that day, the pastor—who did wood carving—had cut a long-stemmed chalice from Ebony wood and had sent it to me to thank us for sharing the word and sacrament with them that day.

## Larger than Legion

On a recent trip we saw extraordinary results, beyond the people who made professions of faith in response to the outreach: I led the group to a far-off, difficult-to-reach place, where no missionaries had ever been. The hunger for the Word was so intense that the group decided that planting a church would be the best way to serve that community. The pastor and translator who accompanied the group told them that there was a pastor available to be sent out there, but the people had nowhere for his family to stay. They had started building a small house but could not purchase the cement, door and window frames or corrugated tin for the roof. In collaboration with their home church, the visiting team got the ball rolling, and within four months of the trip the house was built, and the pastor settled in the newly planted congregation.

The impact of establishing a permanent church in a community where no church had existed cannot be overstated. In America, we may have dozens or hundreds of pastors in a city. We can hardly imagine a community without *any*. But in Africa, just the fact that a permanent pastor has become part of the village has a huge effect. It means God cares for *them*. Regular church services, together with home visitations, changes the dynamics in the community. As the number of believers grows and their faith matures, the message of reconciliation is enhanced. Seeing lives changed before their eyes, the wider community responds with curiosity and interest, which opens the door even wider for further evangelism and mentoring. The fruit gained from entering virgin spiritual territory—or even hostile territory—is sweet, and in most cases low-hanging, at the beginning. The harvest is ripe. Join us in bringing it in!

We came prepared to show the "Jesus Film" to the community on the second night of our visit. People from all over who had heard of the meeting that evening came to the clearing in the bush. We had cut some saplings as the poles for the screen (a sheet we had brought) and wired the projector and sound system to the big, heavy battery we had with us. The indigenous pastor got the people to sing while it got dark enough to start the movie.

These people had never seen a movie. A shout of surprise went up from the crowd when Jesus spoke Nyanja, their language. They sat spellbound until the scene of the storm on the lake (remember, most of them are fishermen who use tree-trunk dug-out boats), the waves coming over the sides of the boat had them screaming in alarm. As the storm abated upon Jesus' command, they calmed down. The very next scene shows the demon-possessed "Legion" coming, in a threatening posture, towards the landed boat with a big rock in his hand.

Jesus locked eyes with Legion, and slowly Legion lowered the stone and backed down. Gasps of amazement flooded the crowd. They were very familiar with manifestations of demonic powers, but they had never seen such a calm way of dealing with one.

Right at that moment, everything went dark as the projector cut out. I frantically searched for what had happened. Finally, we realized that the battery had died. I apologized profusely and promised that we would have another showing if they invited everybody in the entire area. They agreed.

A few of the community leaders came forward to offer their wisdom on what had happened: "That Legion, he was the one who broke the film." And that was that.

Three weeks later my son-in-law and the pastor returned and showed the "Jesus Film" again. More people turned out than before, and they reacted overwhelmingly—everyone attended the church service the next day. We were more than excited that the newly established church, with a new permanent pastor, could get such a start. A few people answering the call on their hearts got the job done, and Legion's plot was more than thwarted when the second audience was much larger than the first.

# ⌃⌃⌃11  REVIVAL, AWARDS, WISDOM, AND BIBLES FOR DISCIPLES

O ne of the tragedies in Africa is that the traditional extended family structures have broken down over the last couple of decades. Encountering single mothers is common and prevalent in the church. At the same time however, people enduring difficult circumstances are generally more open to respond to the gospel. Thus, one of our teaching modules on marriage and family sensitively addresses the issue of Biblical principles for marriage, sex, and the consequences of sin in this regard.

Africans regard Scripture as the inerrant Word of God and accept teaching if clearly shown that it is from the Bible—this is a huge advantage over many western reactions that question the veracity of Scripture. A question such as, "Who says that the Bible is true?" undermines a faith conversation to the point that requires first establishing another base of common ground before any possibility of constructive dialogue is possible. For example, "Truth" for some in our culture is absolute—

firm, unchanging, something you can set store by—and for others, it is relative—influenced by circumstance or mood. When called to teach and guide leaders in the faith realm, it is most important to espouse and understand how to transfer strong, clear, unchanging, and defining principles to them so they can disciple followers. In our course materials, definitions for Christian and Bible terminology play a significant role. We have found that the depth of understanding of the principles profoundly influences the strength, endurance, and longevity in faith—of the respondents who have experienced rebirth—a spiritual revival from a spiritual death brought on by sin, Col 1:13 &14 *"He has delivered us from the domain of darkness and transferred us to the kingdom of his beloved Son, in whom we have redemption, the forgiveness of sins."*

We often hear church members pray for *revival*. What do they envision would be the answer to their prayer? The picture conjured up in many minds by this concept is a huge crowd, possibly swaying in worship, where many come under a conviction of sin, repent, receive forgiveness—and then go on with their lives. In extraordinary circumstances, the above happens, and *lives* are permanently changed. Praise God for such great times of awakening.

Far more to be pursued is a personal rebirth by the Spirit of God, a testimony that leads to a personal relationship with Christ. From what we have learned in Africa, it can best be expressed as a person hearing, understanding and accepting God's will for them and then *doing* it under the guidance of the Holy Spirit. That is why the following graduation ceremony stories are precious to me.

## Astounding graduation ceremonies

Graduation ceremonies are always great times of joy for these rural leaders who may never have attended any such celebration. Often they held surprises for us:

- When we arrived in Maputo, Mozambique for a diploma ceremony, we did not understand why there was a procession of some seventy students (with their spouses) lined up to walk through a Gazebo. It turns out that during the classes many of the students realized that they had been married in a traditional tribal ceremony, but not "in church." Their interpretation was, "We are married before the state but not before God—we need to fix that." This was their conclusion after learning that God instituted marriage. So, they decided to have a mass church wedding before the diploma ceremony. Later, many of them testified that their marriages and lives changed entirely from that time onward.

- Two guests, one from England, accompanied me to a diploma ceremony in the Tswana tribal area. Everything went off well, and everybody was excited to see the enthusiasm of the students and their families. As we walked out of the church, we were directed into a home for lunch. Consternation could be seen on the faces of my guests when the meat dish was put before us. It was a traditional Tswana delicacy—grilled chicken feet wrapped with intestines (grilled to a crisp like bacon). I grew up among the Tswana, so for me, it was not a shock at all. I could not help myself—I leaned over to Jonathan and asked whether I could dish up for him. Shocked, he looked at me asking if I was going to eat. "Yes," I replied, and he retorted, "If you expect me to eat that you will get it back with interest." I was able to explain to our hosts that the visitors were not being disrespectful but would prefer some of the chicken carcass meat. They promptly served the meat, and everybody went away satisfied.

- A church choir was invited by the tutor to participate in the festivities where 14 pastors were to graduate from the pastoral course. It was noticeable that the lady leading them remained seated while the rest were standing and dancing to the beat of the accompanying drum. She had a magnificent voice. The attendees applauded enthusiastically after each of the songs. I was curious because her not standing up was counter to the culture. After the ceremony was over the tutor said he wanted to introduce me to her.

I then realized she had had polio as a small child and therefore could not use her legs because she did not have braces. I complimented her on her singing and the way she had prepared the choir for that ceremony. She was shy or just humble in thanking us for the opportunity to sing at such a "big event." She had pads of wood on her knees and hands allowing her to crawl. I was not ready for what I heard next—to attend that service she had crawled 12 miles. We had left our vehicle at the "road" and had walked the final two miles to the meeting, so could not give her a ride. From out of the bush came her voice singing praises to the Lord as she crawled home.

I praise God that He called me to labor amongst such "simple people" who did not have any pretenses and loved Him with all their hearts. I submit to you that anybody ready to walk miles to attend a church regularly is serious about their faith.

## Awards

Africans sing beautifully. They are masters of harmony, and they love to sing a capella. Combining their love for singing and our goal of enhancing their knowledge of the word, we organized choir competitions. Judging the performances followed three criteria:

- Overall sound—Voice quality, clarity and harmonizing;
- Quality of message carried in song—did the lyrics contain the Christian message clearly, succinctly on an easily learned melody;
- Dress and movements to the rhythm of the song.

The enthusiasm with which they approached preparations for the competition and their performances were infectious. The winning choir becomes the custodian of a floating trophy for a year, and each member receives a small personal trophy to keep.

Congregations learn the songs, and thousands of people who do not have access to a Bible or who are not readers can then sing the gospel message. Our goals of propagating the gospel message and teaching the word to congregations, through song, succeed very well.

## Wisdom

So often wisdom is sought where intellectuals dwell, while less-educated people are looked down upon. The following experiences taught me that this is not necessarily always true. It is even more remarkable that the following two encounters took place among people facing the most depressing poverty, suffering, and lack of education. Despite the difficult circumstances, the perspectives of Christ shone clearly in the wisdom living in the hearts of these simple people.

Our Malawi country coordinator, the guide from the church who had come to meet us, and I drove our 4 x 4 vehicle as close as we could get to the church on the Mozambican border. There we planned to meet and encourage a number of pastors from the surrounding area. We wanted to learn what their most significant needs were, and how we could help them.

Mozambique had been claimed by the Portuguese ever since the voyage of Vasco da Gama in 1498. The country was developed and ruled by the Portuguese. But in the tide of nationalism and independence that swept the world following WW II, a protracted insurrection, lasting from 1977 to 1992, forced the Portuguese out. Though the world powers reinforced the nationalist movement, it was led by communist-backed guerrillas. After gaining control of the country, the communist-led government then turned on the tribal groups in the north, who had been left out of the negotiation process for "peace."

The communist soldiers served without pay because the communist government was broke. So they confiscated supplies from the people, and Christians were their favorite targets. Besides being more disciplined and productive, Christians also were considered subversive to the communist principles. So they were targeted and severely persecuted. In fact, the pastor of the congregation we were visiting had been imprisoned. As we walked the rest of the way towards the church, the lead elder told another story of their plight.

"Only last Wednesday night a raiding party came through and burned homes in the village after ransacking any food and valuables they could find," he said.

Following the cultural tradition, our arrival outside the village had to be announced to the chief of that area. Knowing of our appointment, he would be in the village conducting official business until we arrived. If he were busy with a court case, we would have to wait for him to call for a recess at the first convenient time in those proceedings before officially greeting his visitors. This is standard protocol and would be repeated when we were ready to leave at the conclusion of our visit.

Our host, the lead elder, was clothed in a bright white shirt and Sunday pants. We later learned he had borrowed the clothes from a friend in another village. What he still owned, after the raid, was "not thought to be adequate to receive visitors." African Christians always receive visitors in the best manner they can. He displayed an equally bright smile as he welcomed us at the church. He gave us details of their situation over the period when fighting between the two armies had come into their district. They had previously suffered a lot, but the raid of the previous week had been the worst they had yet experienced.

"The soldiers grabbed everything from our homes," He began. "What the soldiers could not carry they loaded onto the backs of young women and commanded them to follow the soldiers to their temporary camp. They cut off one earlobe of each of these girls to mark them as slaves."

"We were stunned. We tried to comfort one another while crying out to God for protection against further harm in the village and grieving over the girls who were taken away. Would we ever see them again? We desperately prayed our Heavenly Father would return them.

"At that moment, a chicken came strutting into the village from out of the grass. The raiders had not found her. We, the entire congregation came together to worship God over that one chicken. It gave us hope that God had heard our prayers."

I had the opportunity to speak with the elder's wife—not something that happens too often, since ladies usually are busy serving the guests. She told me, "My husband and I ran for our lives to get away from the soldiers. We left everything behind. When we were sure that the soldiers were no longer chasing us, we stopped and hid in the undergrowth. As we looked back towards the village, we saw our home burning from the fires set by the soldiers. What else could we do? We fell on our knees and thanked God for our escape. Then we prayed and *forgave* the soldiers." (She emphasized *forgave*.)

I naively asked why she so strongly emphasized forgiving the soldiers. Her answer has stayed with me to this day: "We have learned that God does not live in a heart where there is no peace or where unforgiveness is present!" Their simple faith, dedication, and trust in God still amaze me.

The other pastors recounted the stories of the persecution they had suffered at the hands of soldiers, but none were as bad as the one described above. After doing what we had come for and making ready to leave, it did not strike us as strange that they asked us to wait. I assumed that the Chief was not available to see us off at that moment. I was not ready for what happened next.

As we sat in the shade of the hut, a woman came carrying a pot which she set down before us. They had slaughtered that surviving chicken and prepared it for us as their guests! I protested that I did not need their only food, but had no choice when they replied, through the interpreter, "We prayed to God that He would send us His representatives and now you are here. We have made this sacrifice to God in thanksgiving for hearing our prayer. We cannot eat the sacrifice, but you are God's representative to whom we are giving it." The portion of chicken I ate that day made me understand that these simple people understood *relationship* with Christ far beyond my understanding. I had also not seen *love* for God and fellow man like this before.

The war moved out of that area not too long after our visit. We were able to deliver most of the needed items we had discussed with the leaders, and most of the girls did return to the village soon after our visit. There was great rejoicing in the camp.

## Shire River Valley

During the civil war in Mozambique, many refugees crossed the Shire River into Malawi to get away from suffering the consequences of being caught in the crossfire. Willie and I went into the valley to assess the situation there, since more people who needed to be reached were coming across the river.

Although Nsanje is a long way inland, it is not much above sea level. Thus, the Shire River valley has a tropical climate, hot and very humid. The soil is reasonably fertile with a dense growth of shrubs and undergrowth limiting air flow—its "comfort index" is very low.

We had brought Bibles to distribute through the churches we were working with to new believers responding to the evangelism outreaches among the refugees. At the point where our 4-wheel-drive truck could go no farther, members of the churches targeted for delivery met us. It was quite a long way to the distribution point but carrying a box of Bibles on each shoulder was the only solution. A particular type of grass (about 6 ft. tall along the footpath) has a thorn-like tip and brushing against it cannot be avoided as the path is narrow. With the heat causing the blood vessels just below the skin to open for heat exchange to keep regulate the body temperatures, any contact with sharp points causes some bleeding. None of us noticed anything until we put the boxes down and someone said, "Look how much they love us, they are shedding blood to bring us Bibles."

Having expended all my energy, combined with the heat and humid air, my world was "swaying." I sauntered over to some shade, sat down, and realized that I was on the verge of fainting. A woman working over her cooking fire saw what was happening, recognized my vulnerability, and quickly brought a cup over to me gesturing that I should drink. I did not know what it was, but I felt lame and floating and was desperate enough to try anything. It was tea brewed with goat's milk with syrup extracted from sugar cane by pounding it in a mortar and pestle. The sweet, rich, creamy brew did the trick. I regained focus and within a short time was able to continue participating in the meal the woman at the fire had prepared.

Amazingly, she worked over that fire in the oppressive heat of the day with a smile that belied the discomfort she must have experienced. After she brought the dishes of food for us to serve ourselves from, she prayed over the table with humble sincerity for God's blessing on our food and time with them. She could not read or write, and when identifying signatures were required she provided them with a thumbprint. But her wisdom grown by life experience benefitted me greatly that day.

## Bibles for Disciples

Early on we realized that another key element was missing. There was an acute shortage of Bibles. This explained the reason for the deficit in competent leadership within the rural village churches. In official reports, Bible Societies and suppliers conservatively estimated that some 200 million Christians on the African Continent do not have access to a Bible—staggering numbers. We found many congregations where there were only a few Bibles, even some churches where there were none, not even for the pastor.

Being associated with Open Doors with Brother Andrew, and particularly on the prayer team for a Bible project in 1981, sparked my passion for making sure that Bibles are available to Christians. God answered the prayers of thousands of His children who were interceding for Project Pearl: procuring and delivering 1 million Bibles into China. It was an experience I will not forget: the emotionally charged atmosphere of joining the insider prayer team for such a vast project, rising emotions as we became aware of how ambitious the undertaking was, knowing that very few people knew of the upcoming delivery. Our sense of excitement heightened when the green light was given, and reports reached us of the successful delivery to Christians inside China, and of the safe return of the brothers who had physically done the delivery. The joy was overwhelming when we realized that the Lord had honored His guidance to obedient men. The flame that ignited in me to provide Bibles, the objective truth of God, into the hands of His disciples still burns brightly today.

Two incidences in Malawi will remain with me as long as I live. Remember that for years Malawi was the most impoverished country in the world, and a Bible could cost up to a year's cash income for a family.

One of the pastoral students stood out among the groups who had completed their three years of study and were graduating. His hair was almost pure white—not something you see too often. In some parts of Africa, the life expectancy of a man is as low as 37 years. As he came up to receive his Diploma in Ministry, I asked the tutor if he knew what the old bishop's age was. His reply, although not unexpected, was sad, "He does not know when he was born." The short testimony, as he received his diploma, was crisp, to the point, and scripturally accurate. "Thank you, Father, for Jesus, Your Son, my Savior."

When I handed him his Bible, he took it, and the tears streamed down his cheeks. He hugged the Bible and then kissed it. He had never had a copy of his own for the full duration of some 38 years that he led his church (and planted many more). At further inquiry, it became clear that he could not read; he called on school children to do the Bible reading for him when preparing his sermon and before he brought his messages to his congregation. He had told the tutor that he could not read in class because the candle or kerosene lamplight was not bright enough. Thus, everybody accommodated his "problem" without digging deeper.

Moral of the story for me: Faithfulness! Would I ever have been faithful, the way he was, to God while not having anything other than God's call on my life? Oral learning, including retaining and being able to render back verbally close to verbatim what they have heard, is the secret behind many very effective evangelists/preachers who have limited reading skills.

I was invited to preach at a small church in an impoverished area where we were researching the reasons for the heavy persecution they experienced. All their Bibles had been confiscated (which I only found out as a result of what happened during the worship time). The pastor spoke in his native language (which I did not understand) and immediately a lady got up and started singing for quite some time. As she "faltered" a man jumped up and continued. I turned to the pastor to ask what was going on. His reply stunned me, "We are showing you that our church *knows* the entire Gospel of John by heart. We need God's word. Because we do not have any Bibles left here, we are learning it this way."

Afterward, I learned that the pastor would walk for a couple of days to another pastor's house where there was a Bible. He would read the next portion of the gospel narrative and learn it by heart. Walking back home, he would set the words to a tune to remember it. On Sundays, he would teach his congregation the "song." Thus, they could quote the Gospel of John verbatim!

Although our Bibles for Disciples project is a never-ending project, there have been times we celebrated God's hand moving mightily as we obeyed His direction. Placing the order for 50,000 Bibles to be printed in a former communist country, because they offered the best price and delivery terms, gave me quite a thrill. We had taken Bibles into Communist countries where Bibles were destroyed as "contraband" earlier. Now the communists were supplying them to us! I did not mind paying them for the printing. I do love it when God's humor is so clearly on display.

In contrast to experiencing God's miraculous humor when providing Bibles, we sometimes endure the fierce resistance of the enemy of our souls to get the "tools" we use to our students. In the next instance, the "comedy of errors" became (just about) laughable.

We ordered a consignment of study Bibles to be available at the graduation ceremony of a group of our top leader students in Zambia. Transport from an Atlanta warehouse to a wharf warehouse in the port city Charleston, SC was arranged, space on the ship booked, paperwork completed, and everything was in place.

Early one morning—days after all was arranged—I got a phone call from a trucker saying that he was ready to deliver the Bibles but needed a physical address as he only had a P.O. Box number. "Where are you?" I asked. "In Waynesboro, Virginia," came the reply. He was ready to deliver the Bibles to my home in Charlottesville, Virginia. Although the address on the paperwork was clearly and correctly documented, he had been told to take the Bibles to the "Invoice address." I refused to accept the delivery because it was not the designated delivery address. The manager of the company called me to secure payment to return the Bibles to Atlanta—again I refused to accommodate their request. "In that case, the consignment can lie in the corner of the warehouse," was his solution.

By then time had run out to get the shipment back to Charleston to be loaded on the ship. However, good news: the ship was docking at Norfolk, Virginia and would accept the load there. I jumped on the phone and told the trucking company of the opportunity to get the load off their necks. Both sides were relieved that a good solution had been reached.

Not so fast. Three days later I got a call from a warehouse in Charlotte, North Carolina asking me what they should do with this consignment that had conflicting delivery instructions. "It was supposed to be delivered to the nearby Port of Norfolk," I replied. "Oh, our trucks follow our routes from Virginia to North Carolina, but we do not have a route directly to Norfolk, VA."

At this point, my patience had come to an abrupt end. The outcome of the ensuing conversation was that the Bibles would be transferred to another carrier, at their cost. I called the wharf warehouse and was told that the ship was docking in two days and that they needed the load as soon as possible. The message was relayed to the truckers, and they were confident that they would make the deadline.

As a precaution, I called the warehouse the next day. "No delivery has been made," was the reply. A call to the truckers confirmed that they had delivered the Bibles. "To what address?" I asked—they gave it to me—it was to the wrong warehouse on the next wharf! I had to sincerely pray for special forgiveness for the anger that spilled over at that point.

The final resolution came when the original warehouse manager sent a forklift to the other warehouse to fetch the load and take it directly to the ship for loading. It was the very last consignment loaded before the ship left port. Thankfully, the final delivery from Durban, South Africa to Lusaka, Zambia went off without a hitch. The Bibles arrived just in time for the graduation ceremony.

In 2011 we drew up strategic plans to place Bibles in the hands of 80,000 believers over the next two years. We had no idea how we would do that, yet our hearts were united on the number. So when we presented the project to our board, it was approved. Much of the distribution was done through the school system in that area. Christian children were given one copy per family with the instruction to tell parents about the training classes that were enrolling people into the disciple-maker groups. The rest were given to our 7,000 pastoral students to use in their congregations as evangelism and discipleship tools.

Because there were so many non-readers in our area of operation, we approached God's Word for the World, which was developing a Bible for children. We were excited about joining with them for the first print run and ordered 35,000 copies of "God's Word for Children." We are developing a Youth Disciple-Maker Program where this Bible will be used extensively. Results of the pilot project in Zimbabwe are very encouraging. We expect this to become a significant project aimed at "winning the next generation for Christ."

Our Bibles for Disciples program is an ongoing project where Christians in affluent places can help make a difference in the lives of needy followers of Christ.

# ^^^ 12

# LONG-DISTANCE TRANSPLANT

n August of 2000, I received a telephone call from Christian Aid, with which Timothy Training Institute had been in relationship for years. The purpose of the call was to ask whether I would consider relocating to the U.S. to be the director of their activities to the African continent. As the CEO of a large ministry working in six African countries, I faced a huge decision. Many questions needed answers:

- Lida was working; our children were not all out of the home yet. Ilne was in her second year of a four-year degree in nursing at Potchefstroom University for Higher Christian Education. Mareli had been accepted at Pretoria University majoring in music, specializing in flute and piccolo. Hanri would complete twelfth grade in December 2000. How could we leave them behind without "abandoning" them?

- What would we do with our home, rent or sell? In either case, would we have to sell our furniture and household goods? We had heirlooms that had been in our families for more than 180 years.
- What would we do with my aging mother who lived in an apartment adjoining our house?
- What if this whole enterprise does not work out and we have to return to South Africa?
- What could we take with us?
- Could we cope with the differences in culture? How would we make friends, not knowing anybody, and yet having to raise funds, without prerequisite trust relationships?
- Mainly, who had the heart for TTI and could fill my position, keeping the two foundational elements of the calling in place?

From day one Ike, Daniel and I understood the challenge of providing entry-level training. We would open enrollment to people who had very little if any formal schooling. Some of our most talented and effective evangelists developed out of this pool.

While TTI's budget was very tight, who would find the funds to provide training for AIC pastors who could not afford even the meager fees? We subsidized their training, but they had to reimburse us as their church and contributions grew. Maintaining this policy was difficult. Moreover, while pushing for higher educational standards and focusing on students who could pay is standard practice, it could exclude the very people God had called us to serve in the first place. Would the program survive if I left?

After much prayer, the board released me to travel to the U.S. to meet the people and learn the activities I would be expected to embrace. The interviews, introductions, people I met, and scope of my responsibilities all went well. The calling was confirmed: we would move across the Atlantic Ocean to Virginia. Upon my return home, God's hand in resolving the issues became evident.

∧ ∧ ∧

*Lida's perspective: This was the hardest question we had ever to contend with—Do we pull up roots, move to America, an entirely unfamiliar world; leave two young daughters and all our family behind? Or do we stay where we are comfortable, continue with the work we love, and where we see the Lord touching lives all the time? As we had our devotions one night, we simply asked for an answer. The piece we had to read that night was from Phil 2:19, 20, NLT—"...I hope to send Timothy to you soon for a visit. Then he can cheer me up by telling me how you are getting along. I have no one else like Timothy, who genuinely cares about your welfare." Johan was known in all the areas where TTI was active, as "Ba Timothy" and we knew! I cannot even remember that we read any further that night: We were overwhelmed by such explicit instruction. And when we ran into uncertainties here in America, we could remind the Lord of His clear calling.*

❤ ❤ ❤

The household goods that we could not keep sold "yard-sale style" (not a known concept in South Africa; they prefer auctions). People walked away with "bargains," and stuff from three households (ours, mom's and the rental apartment on our property) found new homes in four days.

Storage for the heirlooms was found.

Our cars sold just days before we boarded the plane to fly out. People we did not know before made it possible for us to entrust our two older daughters to their care for the time they were at the university.

Our plans for Hanri also came together: She would travel with us to the United States, and then return to South Africa to join the Navy. There she would complete her studies as a nurse and serve as such in South Africa.

I flew out in February 2001 to arrange for our living accommodations in the U.S. We agreed to supervise the ministry's guest house in compensation for our lodging. Lida and Hanri arrived in April. Each of us was allowed two travel bags. So, with all that we could fit into six heavy travel bags, the three of us started our life in a foreign land.

Hanri's plans changed dramatically during the year. She later graduated with a nursing degree from Liberty University in Virginia. She met Peter, a young man from the Middle East, and they got married at the end of the year. They continue to minister in his country of origin which is not open to the gospel.

After completing her nursing degree, Ilne worked for two years as a nurse and then applied to work on the Africa Mercy, a hospital ship going to African ports where visiting surgeons performed necessary surgeries. It was then stationed in Liberia, West Africa. There she met Carl, who would become her husband, and they have since served together in ministry in many countries. They currently serve on Nongo Farm near the Zambian town of Mazabuka, where the Dignity Project development is based.

Our talented musician, Mareli, graduated with two fields of focus—teaching music and the performing arts. Her accomplishments included leading the woodwind section of the Johannesburg Symphony Orchestra for many years. She married Nico, an accomplished musician who had his own band but migrated to building a recording studio. From leading worship at their church to producing CD's for Christian artists, to participating in Symphony Concerts, they actively live out their faith.

In April of 2002, our lives changed again, when Christian Aid went through a major management restructuring. Lida and I, as the newest members of the team appointed by the outgoing president, knew that our tenure would be terminated. We were there exactly one year to the day. Our cry to the Lord for direction was answered swiftly when Lance Thollander, founder of Hope Builders International, invited us to join his mission organization, still in the process of final registration. So, we began a new era in which God carried us in His great mercy.

With no financial support, we had to find our feet quickly. We thank God for Lance and his wife, Christie, for John and Jo Ann Lindner, who welcomed us into their home until we could reorganize our lives, and for a few former colleagues who sustained us by prayer.

I had been trying for more than four months to contact a particular philanthropist with no success. Wondering who I could reach, his name popped into my head. On the first attempt, the phone was answered—not by a secretary, but Mr. Olive, himself. I mentioned my mission to speak to him about a project on the island of Zanzibar. He immediately responded with interest and asked when I could meet him at this office in Tennessee. Our appointment was set within the next week. It was cold, but Lida chose to remain in the car and pray while I went inside to the meeting.

I handed Mr. Olive the two-page proposal, and he scanned the figures. He asked some questions about the implementation of the boots-on-the-ground application. Working with trusted indigenous leaders with whom we had had a long relationship appealed to him. He called his secretary, handed her the proposal and said, "Cut a check for the full amount and bring it in for signature."

Out of the blue, his next question had me swallowing for an answer, "How are you supported?" In short, I told him what had happened and that we, in fact, had no support right then. When the secretary stepped into his office, he asked her to bring a check to him. I could not see what he wrote. Handing me the check, he said, "We will fund you for the next twelve months at this level. Work on building your support and in 11 months, call me with the results of your efforts, and we will decide how we can help for one more year."

I did not look at the check until I was in the car with Lida. When we saw the amount, it was enough to sustain us for a full month. We wept together acknowledging that we serve a gracious and all-knowing God. It was then that Lida told me that while praying for the meeting the Lord gave her total peace that He had already intervened.

At that moment, a few things spoken by several great leaders I had served became more than words; they became a reality. If we allow God to work in and through us who obediently follow his guidance:

"You can never out-give God."

"Trust and obey; it's the only way."

"Go is God's command; if you return, it is His grace alone."

"God's provision is always enough."

Eleven months later when I called to schedule the meeting to discuss the level of support they would offer, the secretary seemed distracted and asked whether she could call me back later. The call brought a shocking message. Mr. Olive had come into the office that morning. He did not feel well, collapsed and died right there in his office before medical personnel could get to him.

We were again in a position where we had nowhere to go but to God. Again He undertook through our son-in-law who had the capacity to help for the next few months it took for us to be able to handle the expenses ourselves (with God's provision).

# 13 WELCOME, PARTNERS

I was invited to speak to a group of ten pastors in Making, Kentucky in 2005. They had gathered to discuss possible solutions for the declining church attendance in their region, which they deemed the consequence of lack of trained pastors. The chairman had met me previously, was intrigued with my report of church growth using the Hub Model and invited me to give a 10-minute "Missions Moment."

My little talk created quite a buzz. If primitively trained pastors in Africa saw such growth, could the poor churches in East Kentucky learn from their experience? They suddenly saw new hope for equipping, empowering and encouraging local church leaders to fulfill their calling through Bible training, thus expanding their abilities to grow their congregations exponentially.

Most interesting were the initial responses by two of the pastors who listened to the presentation:

Keith, an overseer of a campground and pastoral counselor-at-large, had the local communities on his mind: "Will this system you described work here?" was his question.

My reply was that the system works when the people you work with desperately *want* answers to their spiritual needs. Results do not come from the system, but from the receptiveness of the *hearts* of people. Keith was serious about testing the model and decided to do something about implementing it amid dire needs of the churches in East Kentucky. The coal mining region holds a multitude of small churches that cannot attract pastors, be it for financial instability of the economy or a host of other reasons.

Keith started Cumberland Area Pulpit Supply (CAPS) and worked hard at inviting leaders from these churches to attend the training seminars on Saturdays. Word-of-mouth spread and invitations to present the workshops in different places forced the team to find and deploy associate trainers to conduct the seminars. CAPS training became so popular and spread so far that some years later I met pastors way down in Tennessee who had been trained in the system.

Jeff, a friend of Keith and pastor of a church in Cornettsville, the second pastor waiting to ask his question, had the uttermost parts of the world on his mind: "Are the numbers you quoted *real*, and can I go and visit them?"

"Yes, when can you go?" I replied.

Jeff invited me to speak at his church the next Sunday morning. He went on a short-term mission outreach the following summer and came back a changed person. After seeing people respond to the spoken gospel message and wanting to expand his walk of faith, He was ready to follow Jesus and pack up and go to Africa.

I had to get him to see the best way required to serve in a part of Africa where there are indigenous leaders who have a call from God but lack the training to reach their own people effectively. If he, a foreigner, went, he would first of all need support to keep himself on the field while he learned the language (or languages) spoken in any defined area. He also would need to adapt to the culture before he could begin building relationships with locals that would allow him the trust to speak into their lives.

I explained our model of working with and through local leaders. Finally, I said, "Jeff, I am not going to allow you to become part of the problem when you can be part of the solution."

Jeff fully understood and inspired his small congregation to begin financially supporting the training of 40 indigenous pastoral leaders in Zambia. A few years later Jeff and I worked together with his church board to plan his release to start working with us on a part-time basis building support for the indigenous leaders who applied for training. He is still working with us in the U.S., and you will hear more of him later. And that small church in Eastern Kentucky is still supporting Hope Builders. They may not have personally gone and preached in Africa, but what a cloud of witnesses they have garnered in sending indigenous workers into the harvest!

# ^^^14 A SECOND GENESIS

L ance Thollander and I continued to operate our separate divisions with utmost harmony. He focused on Asia, and I concentrated on Africa. In 2010 he decided to go a different direction; he wanted to move to Texas to be near his grandchildren. So we decided to separate the ministries. He continued as Hope Builders International, and I took the name Hope Builders Ministries. I was determined to give full attention to our expanding ministry to the African continent.

Just as TTI had separated from Open Doors, everything again had to be set up anew. Dana, my office colleague since our early ministry life in America, handled the transition paperwork and got our new financial system up and running smoothly. From the beginning, she also has been a diligent accountant.

At the same time, the churches in Africa entered a particularly volatile time affecting our church-planting system. I was tired from church infighting and leaders failing to remain humble after receiving their Pastoral Diplomas, and I complained bitterly to the Lord. In short, I was ready to give up.

We knew that the multiplication strategy worked, but unlike the early church described in the book of Acts (and in our first over 20 years of training pastors), a new spirit of assertiveness seemed to have crept into the younger student leaders. Most of it probably stemmed from the demography—the students had become younger over time, and increasingly many aspired to lead and "own" a church. After receiving their diplomas, they did not want to stay accountable to the fellowship for further nurturing and mentoring as was previously the case.

Being called upon to solve interpersonal or relational conflicts in the churches made me feel I had become a "changer of dirty diapers." It was turning my hair grey at a faster pace than I was ready for. It also coincided with a parting of ways with one of our early partners who wanted to expand into areas that Hope Builders did not include in its Vision Statement. The separation was managed well from all sides, and no hard feelings ensued, but the stress of it all weighed me down.

I now point to my grey hair and tell people that each of them (including my beard, which I had to grow to have enough hairs) has the name of a church written on it. However, in the midst of prayers decrying the feelings of failure, a prominent thought came to mind, "Do it My way." I stopped and asked for the guidance of the Holy Spirit as I pondered what this could mean—*I thought we were following Your way, Lord, all this time.*

Looking again at 2 Timothy 2:2 to see if I had missed something there, I prayed for clarity. The crux of what we gleaned was that this model works to the fourth generation of discipleship—Paul to Timothy to faithful men to others. I concluded that we should continue implementing the multiplying model.

The next Scripture that came to mind was Matthew 28:19, 20, "Therefore go and make disciples of all nations, baptizing them in the name of the Father and of the Son and of the Holy Spirit, and teaching them to obey everything I have commanded you. And surely, I am with you always, to the very end of the age" (NIV).

Reading and rereading the Gospels with particular attention to the way our Lord had done ministry, a model started to crystallize for me. So many of the missionary sermons call people to "go." Is that the main objective of the missionary command? Let's test it—If someone *goes* to a foreign country and does not represent Christ well there, is he fulfilling the Great Commission? No. In the same way, we can try to *teach* people, but if they do not learn, or if we *baptize* unregenerate people, we again are not fulfilling the Great Commission. The preeminent goal of the Great Command is "make disciples." All three of these other activities— going, teaching, baptizing—are important, but only as they support the central imperative—make disciples.

Of course, only someone who is born again can be a *disciple* of Jesus Christ (witness, be an ambassador, representative, or do what the Master does). The implications of this fact hit me like a ton of bricks. Where do we see active disciple-making being practiced today? What does it look like? What are the essential ingredients for attaining the successes of the early church? Let's remember that early historians stated that the entire known world knew who Jesus was by the time the Jerusalem temple was destroyed in 70 A.D.

## A new look at discipleship

Studying the way Jesus taught and how the disciples learned, we see that Jesus used parables employing real examples they could see, their cultural knowledge and practices, and more to build their competency. For hands-on experience, He sent His disciples out two-by-two with instructions on what they should do if they were welcomed, or if they weren't. When they returned, He debriefed them, allowed them to share what God had done through them, and corrected and adjusted their message when needed. This apprentice or mentoring model built relationships while teaching them the how, where and when of His vision for the kingdom and their roles in it. He wanted them to be like Him in all aspects, to face the world into which they were being sent. It soon had a profound impact on the world. Under the guidance of the Holy Spirit, they went out and changed the world—because they followed what He had modeled before them.

Another interesting observation was that although Jesus had 12 disciples, He spent a very high percentage of His time with three: Peter, James, and John. He took those three to the raising of Jairus' daughter, the Mount of Transfiguration and Gethsemane. The question: "Whose responsibility it was to tell the other nine disciples what happened?" begged an answer. The answer became clear to me when the words of Acts 1:8 came to mind: Jesus said that His followers would be His *witnesses*. So the task of telling fell to Peter, James, and John.

As soon as this detail fell into place, I was amazed to recognize that the pattern was confirmed as it strengthened—Jesus focused on Peter, James, and John. If they were to each mentor three that would account for the remaining nine. Duplicating the one-on-three pattern becomes very significant if combined with the four generations mentioned in 2 Timothy 2:2 (our original calling).

Were there more pieces of evidence in Scripture to support our developing model of disciple-making? Look at the encounter between the disciples and some Greeks who wanted to meet Jesus. The Greeks approached Phillip and asked if he could take them to Jesus. After all, he was a disciple and therefore had access to the Master. However, Phillip did not take them to Jesus directly. He called on Andrew. Why? It seems reasonable that they were in the same triad, and that they used the principle they had learned of doing ministry two-by-two. The two then took the Greeks to Jesus (John 12:20-22).

The next clue for me came when I saw the numbers of disciples gathered after Jesus had ascended to heaven: Acts 1:15 records that the disciples gathered together in the upper room were 120. I sat and played with the one-on-three multiplier, applied the four generations to it and was amazed at the outcome. First generation = Jesus x 3 = 3 Disciples; second generation 3 x 3 = 9; third generation 9 x 3 = 27 and fourth 27 x 3 = 81; The total adds up to exactly 120 Disciples. Was this a coincidence? Or did our Lord not only give us the gospel message but also modeled the best practical strategic way of effectively accomplishing His will—that none should be lost? The answer lay in testing the theory and measuring the results attained when implementing this strategy.

We chose the Makua tribal region in northern Mozambique to run the pilot project and refine the methods of deployment. It was the most secluded and largest tribe among the less-reached groups in southern Africa. The results could be measured with the least outside influence. Pastor Gerald, an experienced Portuguese-speaking missionary who had led the church planting efforts to the Makua people, was commissioned to implement the pilot project.

Logistically, it was a challenging project for several reasons: limited access (remoteness, bad roads, lack of gas stations); language and literacy limitations; poor infrastructure, and the methods of delivering heavy teaching material. However, we were all expectantly looking forward to assessing the results produced by the interaction between the two multipliers—one-on-three disciple-maker training program extended to the fourth generation.

## Background

Pastor Gerald of a church in Michigan had been a missionary to Brazil years earlier, and ever since had been providing assistance to a Brazilian missionary working with the Makua. For 13 years he had been praying for the Makua tribe in Mozambique. One day he read an article in a

Christian magazine about our Hub Model of church planting. The rapidity with which churches could be planted and pastors trained struck him. He contacted us and consequently became a part of the outreach to the Makua tribe. He identified and equipped a number of tutors in different regions with the hub strategy. From the time he came on board to oversee the work in northern Mozambique, the number of pastors trained and deployed to churches planted had risen to 704.

Pastor Gerald now needed to get those 704 pastors into the Disciple-Maker Program together. He hoped they would understand the mechanics of the new program and be able to deploy it in each of their congregations. In regional conferences, pastors practiced the disciple-maker procedures with which they hoped to disciple their second-tier leaders—elders, stewards, deacons, choir and youth leaders—or whatever kind of leaders they had.

The pastor is the overseeing mentor and not counted in the DMP student number. At the same time, his overseer role is only one of his congregational duties. He still visits and encourages the members of his church as he guides the disciples through the course collectively or in smaller groups. The training takes approximately six months. Each of the 24 lessons focuses on equipping the students so that they can start their own disciple-making group. Midway through the course, each student is expected to have prayed over and found three persons to begin a disciple-making relationship with—not just develop a friendship.

We have found that witnessing what God is doing in the disciple-maker's own life produces the best fruit. So the disciple-maker practices what he or she teaches and will do so on a more exposed terrain when they finish training their disciples. Their students are then trained to become witnesses and disciples also.

When the pilot program was done, we would then implement the Great Commission literally as written in Matt 28:19 ff. on all fronts.

Deploying the Disciple-Maker Program to five of the six countries we work in was the next step. Because cultures differ, we expected some resistance to the changes we proposed. It took some adjustments to satisfy pastoral leaders that the shorter course was not a compromise which would put their congregational leaders in competition with them. They feared that younger men who get training might challenge them in the congregations in which they had served for many years.

# 15    LIDA'S LIFE
## CONFERENCE MINISTRY

**H**ordes of people walking everywhere, as well as multitudes of children, is a common sight in Africa. Traditionally it is more important for boys to attend school than for girls. This is because a girl becomes part of her husband's clan, so her earning potential transfers with her. Consequently, few women have leadership roles. In most cases, the wives of pastors in the rural areas are not capable of significantly supporting them in ministry.

So the desire and need for training is easily identified, but there is another problem—culturally a man cannot teach another man's wife. Men are concerned that she may get to know more than they do. That meant we had to find a woman to lead the training.

Because our children were grown, I asked Lida if she would be ready to consider such a role. I knew that she did not care for camping or communal bathrooms, so I was not surprised when she answered, "If there is no shower or porcelain throne, I am not going there." The queen had spoken!

Melinda invited me to speak about missions at a conference she organized. As I got to know her and her husband better through speaking engagements and her leading ladies who came on short-term outreaches, I realized she would be the person who could "rough it" in the bush—her family took camping trips and were comfortable with simple conditions. At first, she felt that she was not capable or equipped to teach women cross-culturally. However, she continued to go on summer outreaches with us.

Then one day she called me and said that God had spoken to her about stepping into part-time ministry to train women. I helped strategize the seminar format, initial curriculum, teaching times, and trip length. Our tutor worked with his pastoral students to allow their wives to come to the seminars. It was a totally new concept for them, so the first series was tough. But it worked, and the women (and the pastors) acknowledged the growing impact the women had on their congregations (the majority of which were women).

After Lida heard Melinda share about the blessings of God on the women's ministry, she became interested in accompanying her. As co-teachers, they were even more effective in mobilizing the wives of leaders in Zambia, Mozambique, Malawi and Tanzania to assist their husbands in growing the church members both in numbers and in spiritual maturity.

When, after seven years of partnership, Melinda decided to start an autonomous ministry, Lida was ready to head up our Regional Disciple-Maker Life Conferences. The 2017 series had Lida co-teach with Lou Ann (Jeff's wife), our daughter Ilne, and Kristen, a lady from our church in Charlottesville, Virginia who accompanied us on a summer outreach. They trained 600 attendees on the six-week trip. We have since promoted a Zambian couple, Mulenga and Lydia, who attended the conferences as translators, to be the resident Zambian coordinators and teachers at the smaller local congregational Life Conferences.

As suspected, this ministry grew faster than any of the other longer-term courses and is a game changer in the bush of Africa. The Disciple-Maker Course we developed, as a follow-up on the Life Conferences, runs over a six-month period, resulting in evangelists equipped to minister to people in their communities, as well as leading them along the first steps on their road to mature Christian faith.

Both outreaches (the summer conferences that Lida presents to the top district leaders and their wives to help them teach the wives of local village pastors, and that of Mulenga and Lydia to respond to pastors who want further equipping in their congregations), are growing exponentially.

^ ^ ^

*Lida's perspective: Recognizing the opportunity presented to me—to go into the rural areas of Africa and teach the women what God had taught me over many years—excited me. Yet I understood that there would be many challenges and many times when I might doubt if I was in the right place. I needed a very clear confirmation of God calling me into this ministry, one that I could hold before Him in hard times and also in times of joy—and, from a human perspective, as success.*

*Paul's word to Titus in chapter 1 verse 1-3 (NLT) confirmed my calling: "I have been sent to proclaim faith to those God has chosen and to teach them to know the truth that shows them how to live godly lives. This truth gives them confidence that they have eternal life, which God—who does not lie—promised them before the world began. And now at just the right time, he has revealed this message, which we announce to everyone. It is by the command of God our Savior that I have been entrusted with this work for him."*

*With this clear command and calling, I could step into this ministry and teach under the authority of Hope Builders, bringing what is on the Lord's heart for the people to learn, to grow by, and to live their lives. To this day it is still such a privilege to do this, to see eyes light up when they see themselves as the Lord sees them, and to hear them thank the Lord for what He is doing for them.*

♥ ♥ ♥

# 16        OUR FAMILY

Lida and I got married on the first Saturday of 1976. Her parents officiated the entire ceremony, father conducting the church service and mother the reception. Their position as the local pastor of a church in a rural town stood them in good stead to do so, as Mom had the ladies of her congregation to help her and Dad had access to the church. The wrinkle in our story came that Dad had accepted the call to a new congregation a four-hour drive away, which meant that they were moving to the new town the Monday after the wedding! We could not leave anything at their home but had to go on honeymoon via our newly rented apartment in the city about three hours in the other direction.

We arrived at our second-floor apartment with our car loaded with wedding gifts and the last of Lida's stuff from the previous town where she lived. There was no elevator in that building. When I got to the top of the stairs, I saw water on the hallway floor, looked down towards our door, and sure enough, the water came from our apartment. I wanted to run, open the door and see what the problem was, but my new "romantic wife" needed to be carried over the threshold into the apartment. As I lifted her and stepped into the water my beach thongs slipped and only jamming my back against the wall stopped me from falling further and dropping her. She found it so funny that she could not stop laughing—the more she did so, the more my anger rose.

The hot water heater's thermostat had malfunctioned, and the water was boiling. The steam escaped and rose to the ceiling where it condensed, formed drops and "rained" to the floor. The falling drops were hot enough to burn my scalp as I went to turn the electric power off. The temperature in the apartment was high—nearly matching my temper.

Fortunately, the route the water took from the bathroom went directly out the front door, so there was not much damage besides my bruised ego. With both of us having worked and lived on our own after completing our education, adapting to married life did not come easily for the first six months. Most people would say that we both have pretty hard heads. But we knew that God had brought us together, and therefore we worked at finding solutions compatible with our professed faith.

When our first daughter, Ilne, was born in the winter of 1979, our lives changed direction. Lida paused her career as a mathematics teacher to raise our children. That turned out to be three daughters in short order, all while I was still in my engineering job.

When Ilne was in 7th grade, Lida returned to teaching at the same village school where the children attended. The girls hated it. Mom was strict, and they heard the grumblings from other children. The education system was under pressure from authorities, which led parents to participate much more directly in reforming the system. The Parent-Teacher Association assumed many responsibilities in order to have greater input on who were appointed as teachers, hiring additional teachers (paid for by the parents) to maintain smaller classes, and other functions. The most important issue for me as a PTA member was the Christian ethic of our school. My experience during the next seven years, five of them as chairman of the PTA, taught us that obedience to Scripture had a very powerful outworking.

Throughout the girls' high-school careers, they enjoyed tuition anchored in Christian tradition—though many forces tried to overturn this in favor of a secular school system. Fortunately, our district did not waver as we resisted the "liberators" who sought to unshackle our children from their heritage and history. We experienced victories while other districts did not, simply because the parents supported us as leaders advocating the retention of our Christian ethic and ethos.

As is traditional in the extended African family, my mother played a significant role in the lives of our children. When Ilne went to high school in the city, it was Mom who met her at the bus stop every day, since Lida could not. Mom would take her (and the others as they transferred to the city school) home, feed them, and be there for whatever they needed while we were away. She was also part of providing a safe, welcoming and nurturing atmosphere for our children to grow in. We bought a small farm just outside Johannesburg so that our children would not be exposed to the many temptations prevalent in neighborhoods where both parents were working, and children had to fend for themselves after school. Lida was offered the position of senior mathematics teacher at a school right next door to the one our daughters were attending, thus the transport problems we had dealt with earlier resolved themselves in a way we would never have imagined.

One of the answers to prayer that is most precious to me was that God honored a pact I made with Him when the call to ministry and living by faith had me on my knees before God. We had told our parents that our children would be educated to the point that they would be as well or better educated than we were. There was only one way for me to go—I had to lay this promise before the Lord because I did not know how we could afford to keep that particular promise of college degrees for each of our three daughters. I cannot say precisely how it came to be, but on the day Mareli graduated with her double degree, and Hanri with hers, we did not have one penny in study debt at all. He more than kept His and my promises!

We are trusting God for all six of our children (daughters and husbands), who are in ministry themselves, and our 11 grandchildren to remain in the faith through their lives. This is God's grace to the descendants of those who love Him and keep His commandments (Exodus 20:6).

∧ ∧ ∧

*Lida's perspective: When Johan wanted his Mom to come and live with us, it was a foreign idea to me to have more than two generations under one roof. Until the Lord spoke in 1 Tim 5:8 (NLT)—"But those who won't care for their relatives, especially those in their own household, have denied the true faith. Such people are worse than unbelievers." We converted the double garage into a one-bedroom apartment for her, and she was a real blessing to our family for 12 years until we moved to the US.*

∨ ∨ ∨

## Twice through the Valley

Lida returned from an eleven-week conference trip in the summer of 2015 with something that grabbed my attention. She told me that for some time she had been feeling uncomfortable when sitting down. Later she discovered a lump on the left side of her abdomen which grew alarmingly fast. She did not say anything to me about it while she was in Zambia, but by the time she got home it was obvious.

Her physician immediately arranged for blood work to be done and made an appointment with an oncologist. The results from the laboratory were inconclusive, suggesting that we had dodged the bullet. Days later we received the news that after more specific tests the diagnosis was that she had a rare, aggressive form of ovarian cancer—a tumor that doubles every 28 days. Surgery was necessary and urgent. Asked whether we wanted a biopsy done, we both replied: "No, let's get the surgery done as soon as possible."

When the surgery took place two weeks later, the size had increased to be as big as a grapefruit. When Lida was comfortably back in her room the doctor came to discuss their findings and further treatments. She told us that incredibly the entire tumor was encapsulated in a sack with only one place where a lesion was developing but had not ruptured. All the sample tissue from around the tumor had tested negative—they felt that they had "got it all." No further treatment would be required unless something showed up in her twice-yearly examinations.

Now, more than three years down the road, Lida's health is as good as it has ever been, and the tests remain negative for any signs of cancer.

Carl and Ilne are running the agricultural training program at Nongo Farm in Zambia. Soon after Ilne gave birth to Isabel, we realized that something was amiss. The baby was spitting up most of the milk she drank; not gaining weight—at three months of age she had barely regained her birth weight. Most troubling, her head was not growing. The situation was dire and, as you can imagine, people all over the world were praying for Isabel.

Three months later Carl and Ilne decided to take her to South Africa (as recommended by a physician) for tests to see if the cause of her health struggles could be determined. Of course, the baby did not yet have a passport or travel documents to leave Zambia or enter South Africa. Carl and Ilne persisted in petitioning government officials and finally got the necessary travel documents. However, upon arrival at the

Johannesburg airport the immigration official informed Ilne that the documentation was only good for entrance but not for exiting South Africa or entering Zambia. Getting a passport for little Isabel could take months—a new opportunity for intensive prayer.

For two months, the doctors ordered one test after the other, and the results all came back "normal." Finally, Ilne was told that she could go home (to Zambia) since there was nothing they could do besides genetic testing, which was too inaccurate to consider. But without a passport, Ilne could not go back. Miraculously Carl (a Dutch citizen) informed us all that the Dutch embassy had informed him they had granted Isabel a passport, and it could be picked up at the Dutch Embassy in Pretoria (less than ten miles from where Ilne was staying with Mareli and family). God had answered our prayers again—or so we thought.

Ilne obtained tickets back to Zambia for Thursday afternoon, so glad she was going home. I will never forget when Carl and Ilne spoke to us on the phone and said, "God gave Isabel to us, and we received her with much joy. We are going to love her just as much as our other three kids and will do whatever the Lord shows us is needed for her." We concurred.

A therapist to whom Isabel was assigned, suggested one last test after seeing Isabel regurgitate. The test was done, and the results came back as normal. The radiologist was not convinced and kept reviewing the results. She eventually contacted the pediatrician and suggested that there was a possible abnormality. The pediatrician contacted a surgeon, and he requested an immediate appointment with Isabel. Although his office was closed on Saturday, Ilne was told to bring Isabel in to see him immediately. He prodded, asked some questions, looked up and said, "I am operating on her on Thursday."

On Monday morning, their medical insurance replied to Ilne's request for permission to do the surgery "denied on the grounds of it being a congenital condition." She called me and gave me the devastating news. My reply was that I would call the "family" to see what they could do. Four hours after sending out an email to our Christian brothers and sisters who had been praying with us, and three telephone calls to specific friends, I was able to let Ilne know that the funds would be available and we could wire-transfer the full amount that evening. How much greater is our God than what our small faith sometimes allows us to believe!

Surgery started with a laparoscopy because it was impossible to make a conclusive diagnosis from the tests. The doctor's suspicions were confirmed.

The condition is called "mal-rotation" of the intestinal system which causes failure of the gut and organs to attach to the abdominal cavity; thus "folds" obstruct the passage of food. The surgeon removed, turned, replaced and reattached everything where it was supposed to go, and closed her up.

Isabel lost one year in her development phase, and she is slowly developing. Over the last year, it has become clear that she has suffered some permanent developmental damage. As a family, we have the privilege of seeing her progress as the answer to prayer while we look forward to seeing God's grace abound as He uses her for His glory.

# 17 NONGO FARMS
# THE DIGNITY PROJECT

**W**hat started as an outreach to widows and orphans, the Dignity Project has grown into a much larger operation. At first, our goal was to get pastors to assign 3 to 5 orphans to a widow. We would equip her with gardening tools and vegetable seed so that she can work on a piece of land (near the church) to grow food for her and the kids, rather than foraging in the refuse dump or begging.

As the program grew, we realized the need for training pastors in better agricultural practices. They could not only teach the widows in their congregations to care for themselves and the orphans assigned to them but improve their own harvests as well. The first such training center was started in the Mazabuka district of Zambia, on a 20-acre piece of land that we called Nongo Farm. Nongo, in the local Tonga language means "clay pot" and refers to the widow's pot of oil that did not run out. The local chief assigned us the land so we could teach agricultural practices to local farmers and leaders who implemented the Dignity Project in their churches.

The first big job was to identify missionaries who would be prepared to go and live out in the bush where they would be off the electrical grid, need to start a program from scratch, and enjoy the privilege of finding the resources to support their family on the mission field.

A couple who had served on the Mercy Ships, had built an orphanage in Liberia and had worked in a safe-house for at-risk children in South Africa expressed their interest. The approach and the responses were very sensitive because they were my son-in-law Carl and oldest daughter Ilne with their (then) three small children. We were in the clear to go ahead when God confirmed to both sides that the call was from Him.

First on the multitask list was renovating an old two-roomed schoolhouse into a residence for the missionaries who would head up the program. Carl arrived first and installed doors and windows to secure that part of the premises before the family arrived.

Carl and Ilne both worked extremely hard to get the initial Nongo Farm into a reproducible model. We wanted to reproduce them where the needs are highest and where the biggest returns, in Kingdom terms, could be realized. At the same time, we wanted to develop the capacity of farmers in the communities to serve the local community's food needs.

The training had (and has) many aspects:

- Improve the soil and crop yields.
- We teach the people to compost the plant material left after harvest instead of burning it. The people learn to spread the composted grass cuttings and corral manure after preparing the soil and before planting the improved seeds acquired in bulk by our ministry.
- Emphasize vegetable gardening to provide families with the nutrition they need.

- Teach care of fruit trees and the benefits of adding fruit to their diets.
- Encourage broiler chicken and egg production. Raising chickens maximizes the use of locally available resources.
- Develop animal husbandry. We use rabbits to teach the basic principles of caring for other animals—such as goats and cattle.
- Introduce beekeeping. Ilne (5 ft. tall) looks too funny suited up for the job (especially next to her 6ft. 4 in. husband), whose pant legs barely reach his ankles.

We also had to bring in a lot of machinery to make the most use of a variety of crops. We brought in a tractor and implements to cultivate the land, a shelling machine for the corn, a hammer mill to produce cornmeal, a soya-bean oil-extracting machine, solar panels to generate some measure of electricity, batteries and heating system. All the buildings, including the student accommodations and training facilities, are Carl's handiwork. Their dedication to their calling, despite many hardships, continues to inspire their supporters.

Of utmost importance is to emphasize three significant areas of development this strategy brings into the local community:

- Making use of locally available raw materials (manure, grass cuttings, other plant leftovers after harvesting, labor to "turn" the compost pile) the cost of increasing their productivity is negligible while the increase in yields are very significant—up to 100% in many cases! This means that only a small amount of start-up funding from outside donors is needed to promote self-support significantly.
- Because the participants in the small farmer program physically work alongside Carl and Ilne they "own" the results of their labor. They see the difference in the growth and yields on Nongo

when compared to their own field crops. This can present some skepticism in their minds—such as, what else have you done at Nongo ("other than what we have seen you do—composting, which we cannot believe makes such a difference")?

Another factor is that of limiting the "losses" to crops. For instance, the farmers dry their corn in open wooden pole and wire mesh structures that serve as silo. They are not animal or vermin proof. This means that a substantial percentage (can approach 40%) of the crop is lost having been contaminated or eaten by such.

Hope Builders Ministries has built a warehouse with the capacity of storing 400 tons of corn in bags, which is vermin proof. Participating farmers can "rent" space by paying 1 bag of corn for every 30 stored until they come and fetch it. HBM also organized the purchase and set up a corn grinder at Nongo by getting contributions of corn from the farmers and selling it to pay for the mill. Thus the farmers "own" the mill and get their milling done at a lower rate than non-participants in the program. This has become a sought-after way for the farmers to reap benefits from their equipment providing a service to the local community.

- Working with local pastors the product received from such "charges" are distributed to orphans and widows in the local communities.

# ⌃⌃⌃18  A GALLERY OF LEADERS

**W**ith the Disciple-Making Program (DMP) running well amongst the Makua people, it was logical to expand the program to the rest of Mozambique. Reverend David coordinates the work already being done in this challenging country. David is a level-headed, easy-going trainer who gets things done by encouraging pastors to see the benefits these changes would have for them if they let the Holy Spirit direct them in the process of implementation in their communities. Therefore deployment of the DMP is progressing quite smoothly, and the results are beyond our expectations.

## Invading the prisons

Mechaq, a young graduate from our pastor program, did not want to follow the usual path to become a pastor of a congregation. He had a conviction that God was calling him into "Prison Ministry."

We had no access to government-run facilities, so David advised him to go to one of the rural regional village prisons to ask for permission to speak to the prisoners. Mechaq went to a facility for inmates of "less serious crimes" ranging from petty theft to rape. After days of negotiating, authorities granted him a temporary three-hour session on Wednesdays.

During his studies, Mechaq had embraced the one-on-three multiplying evangelism principle. With David's help, Mechaq drew up a plan and submitted it to the authorities. He believed Christians were incarcerated there. If he found any, he would have personal time with them. He asked for and was granted more time, by the authorities, to do so. Mechaq chose and coached five leaders to use the curriculum, making sure they understood and agreed to teach the lessons accurately. In turn, each of the five disciples would find three with whom they could share the gospel. So the inmates heard Mechaq expound the Scripture each Wednesday, and they then shared with their apprentices on a daily basis what being a follower of Christ is all about.

Mechaq figured out that if he could get into one prison he could get into more—after all, there are five days in every week. It took a while, but he eventually gained access to five prisons in that province. He implemented the same strategy in each one, using the same methods. Every day he went to a different prison in a 170-mile circuit. Many times there was no public transportation, so he hitched rides from passing vehicles or walked. God provided us funds to buy him a motorcycle, and later, Osvaldo, another pastoral graduate, came alongside Mechaq to bear some of the load.

At the end of the first year of prison work, David got a call from the Superintendent of Corrections in the province asking him to attend a meeting with Mechaq on a specific day. The reason for the meeting became evident when one after the other, the Wardens at each of the Provincial prisons gave their reports. Five reported that they no longer knew what to do with their inmates—fighting had stopped; chores were done better than ever before, and disobedience and belligerence were no longer problems.

### Revival inside the walls

Having been in some challenging situations over the years and seen God's hand move in our favor, not too much gets me excited from the perspective of "fear"—stupidity is not something to be entertained lightly. This one got my attention:

With the huge impact the DMP was having in the prisons, David and I were invited to meet the district commissioner and some top brass at one of the prisons where there were 87 inmates. After pleasantries, they introduced their plan. We would all go into the general assembly area where all the inmates would gather. We would be introduced as the people providing the program so that the inmates could "thank us." I quietly mentioned to David that I did not think this was a good idea, "There will be two high officials from the corrections headquarters, two foreigners, the chief warden and two chaplains (from nearby prisons) in there. What if the inmates decide that they had a valuable bargaining chip by grabbing us as hostages." David understood, but said he thought we would be fine. Not getting the support I needed I mentioned my concern to the officials—they smiled and promised that they had a surprise for us. This did not make me feel any better when the heavy steel door shut behind us with an ominous clang.

I was not ready for what happened next. As we filed into the secure area, the "students" broke out in a praise hymn that Mechaq had taught them. They stood bolt upright and belted out the song with joy. What the warden had reported became obvious—we were facing 87 men who had had an encounter with Jesus Christ. Their testimonies that followed bore this out in great measure. They related their "before and after meeting Jesus" stories with such clarity, it confirmed the definition of "revival" that Africa had taught us over the years: each soul reborn by the Holy Spirit constitutes revival as it grows in obedience to the directives of the Spirit of God.

The concession arranged by Mechaq for inmates to grow fresh vegetables within the security walls was another great success. We supplied the seed. It enabled the inmates to channel their energy away from physical confrontations with one another, and it creatively and practically helped them to live out their new-found faith. Remember, the only sustenance and necessities prisoners get are brought by friends or relatives.

By identifying pastors who lived close to these prisons and had a heart for serving the inmates, we have been able to expand the program to 12 prisons. The Secretary of Corrections for the entire country has officially asked us to implement the DMP in all their prisons. We are not able to do so immediately but are working at serving in more prisons as resources become available.

### Discipling many nations

In an amazing way, God opened the door for us to expand our work in Zimbabwe, also. An advocate for another ministry needed Bibles in the Shona language, but there were none available in any Bible society. Somehow, he found an article on the internet reporting that Shona Bibles had been printed privately, and he called me to find out whether I could help him get some. I replied that I could, and from there the conversation expanded.

A year later I was asked to attend their board meeting as they suspected that something corrupt was up with the reporting they received. Being unfamiliar with African culture, they needed advice. I was able to help redeem the project, and it now runs as an HBM outreach.

Zimbabwe is a difficult country to work in; the mood towards Christians is constantly in a state of flux. So I have to deal with ministry *continuity* regularly. Through adversity, God has given us three capable, loyal, resourceful and talented tutors, who maintain continuity and perform above expectations. All three work under David's watchful eye.

David also oversees the re-establishment of our work in Malawi after a succession of droughts and floods left widespread devastation. Our students had to relocate and were not able to attend training classes. It will take a long time to rebuild since it is still one of the poorest areas on the continent. Yet with God's grace we have the basic elements and people in place to press forward.

Southeast Zambia borders Malawi and Zimbabwe, so it's natural that David would direct the work with our local partners there. Many churches are embracing the DMP method to bring the message in a creative way to their communities.

Jeff and his management team in Zambia run the most extensive outreach in Hope Builders Ministries. At the height of the program we had 7,600 pastoral students spread over the three-year diploma course. By encouraging many of our former students (now pastors) to implement the DMP in their congregations, we are seeing exponential growth taking place.

I have not used the names of our indigenous leaders in any of the countries we work in now, and I do not want to show favoritism to anybody, but it would be an omission on my part if I did not mention Matthew, our country coordinator for Zambia, in the same breath with Jeff. Between them, they have worked tirelessly at managing and facilitating the presentation of our work through some tough times. Churches that invite them are blessed to be witnesses of what God is doing in the ministry fields He has called them to serve in.

Although Hope Builders focusses on Africa, a church interested in supporting the ministry in Zambia had an existing outreach in India. They were interested in having the DMP model introduced to their project there. We agreed, and two tutors working in three provinces in India are now experiencing phenomenal results. They reach out into communities through equipping, empowering and encouraging local Christian leaders using the HBM model: making disciples who make disciples to the fourth generation. Although travel to meet with them has not yet been possible due to the government's reluctance to grant us a visa to enter India, Jeff is keeping them going through communication lines.

Blaine, a U.S. Army Afghanistan veteran with a heart for Democratic Republic of Congo (DRC), is the newest addition. From day one he has approached the work with compassionate accuracy for what needs to be done. He knows that *needs* and *wants* are not the same, and our calling is to address the *needs*. Exceptional circumstances exist with travel for foreigners, so we thank God for providing a Congolese pastor to work alongside Blaine to get the different training programs deployed.

Steve, a pastor (now retired) from Michigan, took up the role of senior trainer some years back when he started traveling to Zambia to present seminars on further education to our regional and district leaders. They, in turn, take the lessons back to their students. The feedback from the leaders attending the seminars affirms their effectiveness when the fruits are evaluated by what the local pastor-students report. One attendee said, "Pastor Steve, we are thankful for you all. We will teach our people exactly as you taught us. These words will go out to thousands."

The significance of equipping indigenous leaders to empower their students to spread the word cannot be overstated.

# ^^^ 19      FRUIT OF OUR LABOR

I n a very material world where success is measured mostly in volumes, sizes or numbers, the temptation to use such measurements as bragging rights can entice us to focus on them. Instant gratification is another avenue where many good intentions lie ruined or dead. Therefore, we need to get into a position where we can understand God's perspectives on what, where and how to pursue our calling to the full.

From Scripture, it is clear that God has a long-term perspective on Kingdom outcomes. He called Noah to build the ark and to speak to the people of his day about their lives. Through the entire 120 years of building, all Noah got was ridicule—until God closed the door and no one could open it. God is longsuffering with us also. For how long and through how much sin has He been knocking at the door of each one of our hearts? If God's grace and mercy had not been granted and extended over time, humans would not have survived. If God applied instant gratification in the Garden, Adam and Eve, and therefore the whole human race, would have been dead next to the tree in the middle of Eden. All would have been over and done justly. Instead, God's desire is for no one to be estranged from Him. Therefore He instituted the way of salvation through His Son so that whoever believes in Him will be saved.

From that perspective, I want to share in the form of statistics some of the victories we experienced—purely to bring honor to Jesus our Lord, through whom it became possible. These figures reflect nearly 38 years of full-time ministry.

I led Project Timothy and Timothy Training Institute training programs for nearly 17 years. Our volunteer training team grew to almost 300. Each of these volunteer trainers built relationships with student pastors over a period of three years or more. In places where there were no trainers available, we would only start the multiplying process after one of our students graduated from the Diploma Course (in many cases having been in ministry for much longer).

During this time, some 13,000 pastoral students completed and graduated from the course. With only a few exceptions, each of them was either pastoring an existing congregation or planting a new church in villages where no Bible-preaching church existed. The few that did not go into pastoral ministry were deployed as regional overseers of our training. A significant number of our students came to full-blown faith in Jesus Christ during their training period. Their congregations similarly responded and grew as they received clear teaching from the Word.

Nothing gave me greater joy and praise to God than when one of the young men who enrolled in a class in 1986 and graduated in 1989 greeted me in 2003 when he was appointed as Country Coordinator for Malawi by our partner, Harvesters International Ministries. After reaching the highest level that the local rural school could offer—grade 7—he had no hope of ever studying further. Then he—and hundreds of others like him—found us. The dedication of believers who have experienced God's grace at more than one level in their lives inspires me.

Testimonies of gratitude from pastors, church members, choir members, widows, orphans, inmates, government officials, and supporting partners in the ministry abound. I cannot share all of them individually, but I trust the stories told in this book will give you a sampling of their response. I enjoyed serving them together with the teams God provided.

Much has happened in the last 17 years since Lida and I arrived in Charlottesville. Concentrating on finding support for the work in Africa and not having to manage the field outreaches directly has borne fruit. We have seen God's promise to be with us when we left Africa come true—He has not abandoned or forsaken us. Even in the difficult times, His peace has been our comfort.

Hope Builders Ministries in the U.S. has grown from a one-man band with his wife's support to a team of 10 families, including our board members. We understand that God intervened in two specific ways to supply the needs of the people He called us to serve: First, as the budget grew, both in amount and in the scope of each project, we knew that human effort could never have met it. Second, that leading us to the U.S. was His plan, because there is no other nation on the face of the earth with a more generous heart towards missions—not even close!

From day one, Hope Builders Ministries immediately partnered with the local indigenous groups I had led while in Africa. We worked with established relationships; we didn't need to build them. Everything on the mission field kept running without a hitch.

When we reached the point of having 7,600 pastoral students (spread over the three years of the Diploma Course) in training, we went into maintenance mode by limiting the intake of new students. During the peak decade some 2,500 students per year graduated. Most of them were in Zambia.

Around 600,000 Bibles have been distributed to leaders, disciple-makers and new believers. Of that number, some 80,000 were Children's Bibles (also given to non-readers).

The impact on widows and orphans in the Dignity Project is difficult to measure because when the children grow up and move away we lose contact with them. But we know that many lives were saved and changed forever.

And we cannot calculate the number of children served with the Word because their attendance numbers fluctuated every week as kids brought friends to the presentations.

When the Makua Disciple-Maker Pilot Project ended, an astounding 58,000 people were attending teaching sessions at 704 churches where the program was deployed. Since then the growth has continued; eighteen months later the number of people being discipled grew to 63,000, and the number of churches involved increased to 1,074. Many of these were formed during the pilot phase but were reported only later.

Lida and Steve, a pastor from Michigan who serves as a senior trainer for our top leadership have one thing in common—they invest in equipping the leaders of leaders, yet have very different audiences:

Lida focusses on the wives of pastors and lay-leaders, elders, youth leaders and women in leadership in the churches. By investing in them, a portion of the population that has been "left behind" for generations is now being recognized and helped to play significant roles next to their husbands in the church. They have the capacity of reaching people the pastor would have difficulty touching. This is a very successful project. Ladies walk from 50 to 70 miles away to attend these 2½ day seminars. In fact, the demand has grown to the point where a Zambian couple has been employed to present these seminars year-round.

Steve provides further Biblical training (beyond the pastoral training course) to our regional and district leaders so that they may be more effective as they lead the tutors and trainers under their supervision.

Those who attend Steve's seminars all think it is "the best thing since sliced bread."

Through both, vast numbers of Christians are being equipped and empowered to reach their local communities with the Gospel.

# ⌃⌃⌃ 20    THE STORY CONTINUES

**A**lthough this last story happened earlier in my ministry I want to relate it here near the end of the book as an encouragement to those who may want to come to Africa with me as my time in the mission field winds down:

In areas around the big rivers and lakes, fish is a significant source of protein. Fishermen in their tree-trunk dugout canoes can be seen out on the water from early mornings to late at night. They face many dangers (crocodiles and hippos being the most prevalent) as they eke out a meager livelihood. They mostly barter with their fresh or sun-dried fish for products they need—amongst them corn mush, (called pap and not dissimilar to grits, which is the staple diet for everybody), salt and cloth, would be most important. They prepare a small portion of fish or meat, ensuring it has a substantial amount of gravy, into which the ball of pap is dipped before it is popped into their mouths. The ball is rolled in their hands, and if done correctly their hands remain clean of the "dough" that is the consistency of pap.

Whenever they receive guests they always invite them to eat something. They consider it impolite not to offer you something and impolite for the guests to decline. The cultural principle is that before negotiations can start we must first eat together. During times of plenty, it is not too bad; you can pick your way through the dishes that are brought from the fire, taking just a bit. Another activity that makes most Westerners uncomfortable is in the hand-washing before a meal. Women bring a pitcher of water, a bowl, a cup, a piece of soap and a small towel (if they have one—otherwise it is "air dry") to the seated men. They pour some water from the pitcher over the hands, before and after the soaping, catching the excess in the bowl. All this has to be done with the woman's eyes never higher than those of the men they are serving. This is another strong cultural practice that remains in place.

However, arriving in an area where the crops have failed due to lack of rain or floods, the situation is a whole lot trickier. One principle that will always be upheld is they will give you the best they have available. Two instances way out in the most remote bush of Mozambique illustrate this;

People, especially the elderly or very young, were dying of hunger. Emaciated bodies of those who had gone beyond the point of no return were kept in the shade—it is very hot and humid in the low-lying areas of Mozambique. Sunstroke and skin burns are problems for people who come from cooler climates. At one such a village all they had to share with us were leaves from Mango trees that they had cooked in water. Their embarrassment was very evident in the number of times they apologized for not treating us properly.

After another meeting on the same trip, we were discussing what we could do to help when a woman brought in a small pot. From the odor that wafted to my nose from the pot, I realized that whatever was in the pot had been dead for a while. After apologizing for the meager meal, the cover was removed. There was a fish in there. I immediately sent up a prayer of gratitude—the tail of the fish was pointing in my direction. Some useful information in case you do not know this: a fish rots first just behind the head and then further until it is all rotten. We bowed our heads to say grace and when I opened my eyes the head was facing me. My colleague insisted that he had not touched the pot to turn it, but even now I am skeptical of his answer. I asked him because I know that he had been a health inspector before becoming a missionary, so he would know how fish rot!

Experienced missionaries who had worked with people earlier persecuted for their faith explained the moral behind this. You always pray twice in such situations: first the prayer of thanksgiving, and then quietly "Lord I'll get it down if you keep it down." I can testify that God has honored that second prayer for me many times; I have eaten some pretty uninviting foods. Yet in 38 years of going into the bush, I have never had serious intestinal problems while on a trip. I cannot say the same after eating in pretty good restaurants in Western countries— maybe because I did not pray the second prayer?

Is it possible that when God looks at the world today He may be at the point He was in the days of Noah? In Genesis 6:6 (NLT) God expresses His sorrow that He made humans and placed them on the earth—"It broke His heart." We are living in perilous times where outbreaks of pure evil manifest in unlikely events. Believers who walk by *faith* come under attack from all sides, proving that 2 Timothy 3:12 (NLT) is true, "Yes, and everyone who wants to live a godly life in Christ Jesus will suffer persecution."

With this in mind let us take a look at how much countries have changed as the fervor of *practicing* Christian faith has waned. As the influence of the church (and therefore Christians) abates, morals and life values are often questioned and discarded in the name of being "enlightened." Many churches do not experience the *power* of God displayed in answered prayers. Church members lose interest and drift away because the message is not relevant to them—the life of Christ does not surge through their veins, and many feel trapped on the treadmill of a works-based religion.

But God has not changed: His promises remain true, His expressed values remain in place, and He offers each person who receives the gift of salvation a full pardon of sin *plus* removal of our propensity to sin (breaks the power of sin over us). Abiding in Christ (consecrated to Him as Savior *and* Lord) and being a *witness* to what He is doing in and through each of us is the way to *grow* in our faith walk. What moves us forward on our path of advancing in Christlikeness is not one earth-shattering, colossal event; it is being sensitive to the prompting of the Holy Spirit confirming Scripture (the revealed will of God) and then being *obedient* to doing it.

The most direct instruction and authoritative summary of the role that God in Christ has for each of His followers is recorded in 2 Corinthians 5:17 through 6:1 (NLT, emphasis mine):

> This means that anyone who belongs to Christ has become *a new person.* The old life is gone; a new life has begun! And all of this is a gift from God, who brought us back to himself through Christ. And God has given us this *task of reconciling people to him.* For God was in Christ, reconciling the world to himself, no longer counting people's sins against them. And he gave us this wonderful *message of reconciliation.* So we are *Christ's ambassadors; God is making his appeal through us.* We speak for Christ when we plead, "Come back to God!" For God made Christ, who never sinned, to be the offering for our sin, so that we could be made right with God *through Christ.*

*As God's partners, we beg you not to accept this marvelous gift of God's kindness and then ignore it.*

As new creations who understand the gospel message, we have been called to represent God in ministry by declaring the salvation available in Christ (who paid all our sin debts when He said, "It is finished") to all the world. In this endeavor, one disciple can equip, empower and encourage three disciples, who go on to make disciples to the third and fourth generation. The practice can be deployed by yourself, by small groups, and by churches alike. In this way, the great commission can be fulfilled at an astounding rate.

I trust that what you have read affirms that God is still in control and His plan will prevail in the end. Our role is clear: "Go" (can as well be translated "as you are going" or "Wherever you are") and be a *disciple* who *witnesses* to God's greatness in our lives. This is best done by equipping, empowering and encouraging the people God brings over your path to trust and obey Christ as they, in turn, grow into mature disciple-makers.

# ^^^21

# YOUR ROLE
# IN GOD'S STORY

fter hearing Lida or me speak, or after reading a book like this, many people wonder, *What about me? How or where do I fit in?* Some people ask me, "I am praying for God to show me where He wants me in His Kingdom. Can you tell us how to discern His will?" My answer generally follows the pattern below.

Lida and I have built close relationships with many people in the U.S. Some have answered God's call well beyond any sense of duty to sustain us in some special ways through some very trying situations. They just let the resources that God has given them be available to His servants. The following examples may show you how you can take an active role in living out the Great Commission.

These people provided practical solutions that profoundly impacted Hope Builders Ministries while they continued to serve God daily in their jobs and communities. Yet their actions reached the uttermost parts of the world, even though they physically did not go there.

It is possible for every Christian to help carry the gospel of Jesus Christ to distant places by responding compassionately to opportunities God brings us on a daily basis. All that is required is for us to pray about being alert and open to the opportunities that God brings before us, that we will recognize them and then respond as the Spirit of God leads.

1. Discerning God's call and will can be tough, but He who said that He would open the door to those who knock is true to His promise. Personally, I have for a long time followed four principles when facing significant decisions: Ask for the Spirit to guide me to Scripture that would apply to my situation;

2. Pray for God's peace in my heart when I am in line with His will, (or unrest when leaning towards a less satisfactory solution). Usually, I ask for "doors" to be opened or shut as part of this guidance process;

3. Speak to mature Christians (who do not have an agenda in one direction or another on the subject under consideration), who you know are obedient in their walk with Christ, asking them to pray with you and to share their thoughts with you;

4. Seriously consider circumstances to *confirm* the direction of the leading you are experiencing—whether positive or not to your course of thought. Circumstances should not be the determining factor, but they can lend support to your guidance from the other three elements.

So here are some people and how they responded to the call of God:

**Dwight and Irene:** I first encountered bureaucratic red tape just after arriving in the U.S. as a fully documented, legal ministry worker. Because I did not yet have a Social Security number I could not apply for a driver's license or open a bank account. That prevented me from obtaining a car loan, so I could not purchase a car. Neither could I get a cellular phone, and so on. As frustration mounted, I took more time to pray, asking God to break the power the enemy of our souls was exerting (through what I perceived as blocking tactics) that made me feel as if I were not "welcome" in this foreign land.

A colleague introduced me to Dwight (a used car dealer), telling me that he was a very dear brother in Christ and that he would be able to help me overcome some of the sticking points I encountered. He was right—Dwight gave me good advice, which I followed, and slowly I was able to get the needed documents, permits, licenses, insurance and bank account in place.

Then I could look at cars to go on ministry resource-raising trips. Dwight did not generally have vans on his lot. That day he had two just traded in on other vehicles. So when I asked, he pointed me in the direction of the two vans, giving me their details. I opted for the one with lower mileage, liked it and never looked at the other. When we agreed on a price, I told him I would have to call him to confirm my being able to get car financing with the bank. It was arranged, and I called Dwight to confirm the transaction, but I would only be able to come and do the paperwork after work that same day.

In the meantime, an associate sold the van that afternoon before I could return to the lot! When Dwight realized what had happened, he undertook to get me another van like the one I had chosen, to which I answered, "Don't bother." I had been praying that God would protect me from making wrong choices by closing the door to such transactions.

When I went to look at the other van, it was a more luxurious model with leather seats, sunroof, the whole bit. Dwight let me have that van at the same price as the one I had chosen. Many years later Dwight called me to tell me that his aging mother stopped driving and that he wanted Lida and me to have her car. My testimony on this point is that, although nobody in the whole world knew of my dream of owning a particular make, model, and color, when I drove onto the lot to see Dwight's mother's car, it was exactly what I had dreamed of.

God had intervened on behalf of us both on that first occasion. That incident solidified a relationship that has grown well beyond just a friendship. For years now, Dwight has been a faithful supporter and board member for the ministry. In all our years in the U.S., we have never bought any vehicle elsewhere. God has moved Dwight's heart to keep us in vehicles through thick and thin. Praise be to God, our provider!

**John & Jo Ann:** Upon hearing that our services at Christian Aid along with our lodging had been terminated, they immediately opened the doors of their hearts and home to welcome us to stay with them as long as it took for us to find our feet. Some questions swirling in my mind were, "Do we go back to South Africa or stay in the U.S., where we believed God had called us to come and from here serve the ministries in Africa?" "How will we survive without sufficient financial support in this foreign land?" Even if we could find a place to stay, we had no furniture, appliances, and so on. We had come with all we could get into the two suitcases each. That's all we were allowed to bring on the plane.

They carried us through the time of turmoil getting new work permits, finding a new ministry home with a registered charitable organization, and finding personal support to the point where we could work and earn our keep. John and Jo Ann provided the platform from which we were able to re-start in obedience to our calling to be in the U.S. serving the ministries in Africa. Had they not stepped up, we would not have been able to continue serving with Hope Builders Ministries in the U.S.

**Lance & Christie:** I met Lance earlier on my trips to the US to advocate on behalf of Timothy Training Institute. He represented Ministries in Asia and the Middle East for Christian Aid. When I started working there he became my immediate superior; we had a vibrant relationship for the year we worked together. I heard they had a vision of starting their own charitable organization. In fact, near the end of my first year, they had applied to register "Hope Builders International." On the eve of going on vacation, Lida and I visited Lance and Christie and heard they had received notification of HBI's successful application. For some reason I asked Lance whether he would consider having an African outreach added to HBI, and he was positive. This turned out to be of the Lord, since only two days later we were released from CAM. They welcomed us into this brand-new ministry which meant that we could immediately apply for new working visas. Again, God provided all the elements and people, making possible the transition to continue our calling in the U.S.

Over the next nearly nine years we shared many praises and tears as HBI grew with God's favor. When they decided to move to Texas, the African ministry division re-registered under the name Hope Builders Ministries. This meant that we had yet again to go through the stressful rigors of setting up the framework for a new organization. So we repeatedly thanked God for His grace for bringing us into relationship with Lance and Christie, who were instrumental in His hands to bring to fruition so much more than we could imagine.

**Mike & Karen:** While speaking in one of the first churches to invite me to talk about what God was doing in Africa, I met Mike and Karen. They invited me for lunch at their farm the next day. I was treated to a great steak on the grill as we sat on the deck overlooking the pond. It was there that our hearts were knitted together as I shared the "new" approach to missions: equipping and empowering indigenous leaders to reach their own people. Mike and Karen responded to a matching grant opportunity that significantly increased the effectiveness of our ministry. In fact their support has been the most consistent of all the supporters HBM has over more than a decade and a half.

Through the last 16 years, they have organized and hosted meetings and provided their facilities as a base from which we could work in their region. Even though they passed through some tough times, they also never once missed their monthly commitment of financial support.

I will always remember their expressions of compassion for one of our colleagues from Mozambique they hosted while he was on a deputation trip in Georgia. Ezekiel had forgotten a pair of shoes, and Mike found them under the bed in the guest room. He was overcome when he saw that the leather soles of the shoes were worn through and that Ezekiel had inserted loose replacement soles so that they might look "decent" while speaking at groups Karen had organized.

Besides saving us hotel and meal costs by hosting us, and organizing meetings for us, they followed and supported Ezekiel's ministry until he decided to enroll for further studies and thus was no longer directly involved in outreach. Their hospitality and steadfastness helped advance and develop our ministry. They also serve on HBM's Board.

**John & Beth:** Our relationship started a short time after we arrived in the U.S. and continues to date. They not only support our ministry on a personal level but also through their business. There are others who do the same, and for each of them we are very grateful, but John and Beth are the longest-participating supporters on this level. The group I am speaking of here are the precious Ministry Friends I call whenever an unusually large or very urgent expense (generally unforeseen in our budget) crops up. They have bridged many gaps for us over the years.

**Gerald & Miriam and Steve & Janet:** They represent our retired "volunteer" corps. People who fulfill crucial functions in HBM while not receiving a remuneration (other than reimbursement for out-of-pocket expenses) are worth their weight in gold. They are loaded with experience and wisdom and have hearts committed to serving the Lord without the encumbrances of having to look over their shoulders for practical needs; they are free to serve.

You have met both men earlier in the book, as key mentors to our leader/students and trainers. In both cases, the ladies have hosted, fed and cared for traveling missionaries when speakers came to their areas. This is a particularly rewarding way of moving the needle in missions.

**Ed & Karren:** In the ordinary course of our missionary lives, we share, counsel, or answer some difficult questions from people who attend our speaking engagements. Yet we, also, need to be spiritually fed and filled. So Ed and Karren's home became our refuge, our "filling station." They also host regular small group meetings where the word is shared, and discussions are directed at what the Scriptures say about life and how to live it to God's glory. They also make their vacation house on the lake available for short-term stops for missionaries. They support the ministry with all their assets. What a blessing they are to missionaries who are refreshed, restored and spiritually fed.

**John & Nadine and Dave & Jill:** Besides our walk with others on the disciple-maker path, our relationship with these four saints has grown into close family ties where deep, urgent support is found when particularly distressing things happen. Whenever we need people to share our deepest vulnerabilities and frustrations within a secure, loving, understanding, yet corrective environment, such close, interceding friends are precious.

---

My purpose in sharing the roles that these believers play in our lives is not to focus on them but on what they represent. They answer the call of God the same way I did over forty years ago, following the Apostle John's words to Gaius: "You will do well to send them (traveling missionaries) on their way in a manner worthy of God. For they went out for the sake of the Name, accepting nothing from the Gentiles. Therefore we ought to support such men, so that we may be fellow workers in the truth" (3 John vs. 6b-8 NASB). These verses confirm a truth demonstrated many times over in my ministry—the coworkers are as much part of the team as those who are on the front lines. 1 Corinthians 12 reminds me of the many members that comprise the body. And then verse 27 declares, "Now you are the body of Christ, and each one of you is a part of it" (NIV). What an invitation to be on Jesus' team fulfilling His calling!

Each of us has to start somewhere. Please remember that the first prerequisite is to *be*; only after that can we *do*. God wants, first of all, *you* and your simple obedience as His child. He wants you to *be* His child and only then can He be your God. Only after He has *you* will He have an interest in your capabilities, your skills, or your resources. Only then are you fit with your time, talents and treasure to *be* His representatives in this world for which He gave His Son.

Only after the *be* issue is settled can the *do* part take place. Take the first steps into missions by volunteering with a ministry that draws your heart. Then pray and ask God through His Spirit to lead and guide you in His way. You may be pleasantly surprised in the ways that you can serve Him.

Finally, I am reminded of a phrase that I know to be true: God requires our time, talents and treasure. Faithful obedience releases satisfying, long-lasting joy and fruitfulness.

# ABOUT THE AUTHOR

Johan is President of Hope Builders Ministries and lives with his wife, Lida, in Charlottesville, Virginia.

More information and detail about multiplying Evangelism through Disciple-Making can be found at www.hbmin.org.

Morgan James makes all of our titles available
through the Library for All Charity Organization.

www.LibraryForAll.org